Go

Guide to Online Learning

THOMSON
™
PETERSON'S

Australia • Canada • Mexico • Singapore • Spain • United Kingdom • United States

About Thomson Peterson's

Thomson Peterson's (www.petersons.com) is a leading provider of education information and advice, with books and online resources focusing on education search, test preparation, and financial aid. Its Web site offers searchable databases and interactive tools for contacting educational institutions, online practice tests and instruction, and planning tools for securing financial aid. Thomson Peterson's serves 110 million education consumers annually.

For more information, contact Thomson Peterson's, 2000 Lenox Drive, Lawrenceville, NJ 08648; 800-338-3282; or find us on the World Wide Web at www.petersons.com/about.

ISBN 0-7689-1746-8

Printed in Canada

10 9 8 7 6 5 4 3 2 1   08 07 06

First Edition

Contents

Contents

Acknowledgments

Thanks to the many faculty members, administrators, and others who generously shared their time and knowledge of online learning:

Carolyn Baker, Educational Opportunity Directorate
Mary T. Champagne, Duke University
Barry Currier, Concord Law School
Cynthia Davis, University of Maryland University College
John Dutton, North Carolina State University
Charles D. Dziuban, University of Central Florida
Ernest Eugster, University of Denver, University College
Jeff Ian Finlay, Montgomery College
Thomas Flint, Council for Adult and Experiential Learning
Jennifer Freeman, University of Texas System TeleCampus
Robert Froh, New England Association of Schools and
    Colleges
Pat Galagan, American Society for Training and Development
Steven W. Gilbert, The TLT Group
Edward A. Gill, The Art Institute of Pittsburgh Online
Linda Goodwin, Duke University
Duane B. Graddy, Middle Tennessee State University
Gerald Heeger, University of Maryland University College
Dawn Iwamoto, University of Phoenix Online
Janet Johnson, Rio Salado College
Preston Jones, Nova Southeastern University
Nathan Kahl, Stevens Institute of Technology Web Campus
Kim Kelley, University of Maryland University College
Karen L. Kirkendall, University of Illinois at Springfield
Mark Kretovics, Kent State University
Michael P. Lambert, Distance Education and Training Council
Tim Lehmann, Capella University
Karen M. Lesch, Penn State World Campus

Acknowledgments

Andrea C. Martino, University of Maryland University
  College
Cynthia Maxson, Rio Salado College
A. Frank Mayadas, Sloan Foundation
Bridget McGuire, Kaplan University
Lori McNabb, University of Texas System TeleCampus
Jamie P. Merisotis, Institute for Higher Education Policy
Keith W. Miller, University of Illinois at Springfield
Peg R. Miller, University of Central Florida
Mark David Milliron, SAS Institute, Inc.
Brian Mueller, University of Phoenix Online
Vicky Phillips, GetEducated.com
Janet Poley, American Distance Education Consortium
Henry T. Radda, University of Phoenix Online
Jennifer Rees, University of Texas System TeleCampus
Jimmy Reeves, University of North Carolina at Wilmington
Jo Ann Robinson, American Council on Education
Peter A. Rubba, Penn State World Campus
Carol Scarafiotti, Rio Salado College
Ray Schroeder, University of Illinois at Springfield
Claudine SchWeber, University of Maryland University
  College
Susan G. Sharpe, Northern Virginia Community College
Celeste M. Sichenze, American Council on Education
Vernon Smith, Rio Salado College
Barbara Stein, National Education Association
Jenna Templeton, The Art Institute of Pittsburgh Online
Melody Thompson, Pennsylvania State University
Sue Todd, Corporate University Xchange
Thomas W. Wilkinson, Virginia Polytechnic Institute and
  State University
Richard Woodland, Rutgers University, Camden

Acknowledgments

Thanks to the many online learners who took time from their busy schedules to share their views of online learning:

Bill Glenn and Patricia Glenn of Kaplan University

Julio Aira Jr. and John Bohn of Nova Southeastern University

Larry Brittain Keisler of Penn State World Campus

Pami Ahluwalia, James O'Neill, Ryan Smith, and Edwin R. Watkins of the University of Denver, University College

Patti Jennings of the University of Illinois at Springfield

Gwen Washington of the University of Maryland University College

Danny Cohen, Reneé Green, and Amy Kavalewitz of the University of Phoenix Online

Terri Burris, Ronda Henderson, and Steven Yob of Virginia Polytechnic Institute

Part I

WHAT Is Online Learning All About?

Search

Chapter 1 `Go`

The Online Revolution

Class is about to start. However, you are not squeezed into an uncomfortable chair nor are you sitting next to someone who can't stop yawning. There is no whiteboard. No lectern, no desk. In fact, no teacher stands in front of the class.

Instead, you sit in front of your computer, as do the other students in the class, who, incidentally, are scattered all over the world. E-mails in response to the questions the teacher posed last week have been flying back and forth. It has been fascinating to discuss the assignment with other students and to add your observations. You researched the Web sites the teacher suggested as background information for today's class and read the assigned chapters. You got two questions in the mid-week quiz wrong, but since the software used to structure this class immediately graded the test, it showed what you missed and conveniently referenced pages in the textbook for you to review the information and let it better sink in.

Ah, there's Fumiko who just checked in from Japan. You had a productive e-mail exchange in the class chat room a few days ago about the team project you are working on with her and Dan in California. You all came to a dead end on one phase of the problem and e-mailed the instructor about it. He got back to you with an answer yesterday so that cleared that up. Here he comes online, too. You pull up, on your monitor, the graphic he wants to discuss. Class begins. Welcome to online learning.

LEARNING WILL NEVER BE THE SAME

Though online learning is radically changing education today, it actually began in the late 1800s. Farmers, who couldn't leave their fields to learn better crop management, received lessons in the mail. They dutifully did the homework, sent it back, and got the next lesson. That concept has not changed—distance education and now online learning are for people who cannot be or choose not to be in the same physical location as their teachers. What *has* changed is how courses are delivered. The Internet and other advanced technologies have become the primary methods of delivering online learning, although printed correspondence courses, videos, audiotapes, and CDs are still used. But with ever-increasing advances in technology and bandwidth, today's online learners have e-mail, Voice Over Internet Providers (VoIP), real-time audio, and video literally at their fingertips. Other technologies, like computer simulation, are not far off.

The Internet has prompted the rapid growth of online learning. People find it convenient and easy to use in their personal and professional lives, so why not as a way to learn?

· ·

"We had a fiber optic TV set up twenty years ago and it was a hot thing. Students would come to locations to view lectures. Then the Internet came along and changed everything. There was an explosion of courses and distance learning schools."

Jimmy Reeves, Ph.D.
Associate Professor, Chemistry
University of North Carolina at Wilmington

· ·

▶ DEFINING THE BASIC TERMINOLOGY OF ONLINE LEARNING

Asynchronous learning Classes or discussions are not scheduled at a specific time. Students log in when they choose to get assignments, participate in online discussions, or post messages and completed homework.

Blended learning or **hybrid learning** Classes are held both in a campus classroom and online. For instance, students might be required to be in class with the instructor on Monday from 8 to 9 o'clock. On Wednesday, students participate from an off-site computer at the regularly scheduled time. Then students finish up the week's class work on their own and are required to post it by 7 p.m. Friday.

Corporate universities Employee training is conducted by an outside organization.

Correspondence courses Individual or self-guided study courses are delivered by mail or online from an educational institution. Students can proceed through assignments at their own pace within specified time limits. Assignments are written and returned to the institution either by mail or e-mail.

Distance education, distance learning, or **off-site learning** Educational material is delivered to students who are not physically present in a classroom.

Distributed learning Students, teachers, and course content are located in different places. Teaching and learning are not dependent on one time and one place.

Educational technology Online learning is delivered to home computers via Web communication tools, such as VoIP, integrated videos, and graphics.

E-learning, online learning, or **Internet-based learning** Learning, research, teaching, and testing are conducted on the Internet.

Synchronous learning Classes or discussions are held at a specific time. Students are required to attend by logging in at scheduled times, just as they would if they had to come to a classroom.

Text-based learning Learning relies on the written word for both delivery of the course material and student responses.

Virtual university Educational institution offers most, or all, of its courses online. Many virtual universities are for-profit organizations.

HOW ONLINE LEARNING IS CHANGING EDUCATION

As college and university budgets are cut, institutions of higher education are seeking ways to grow enrollment without building classrooms. Online learning is one solution. In the initial online boom in the early 1990s, traditional colleges and universities and for-profit distance education providers flocked to the Internet as a vehicle to deliver courses. Educational institutions recognized that people of all ages were willing to pay for the convenience and flexibility of learning online, and they could now reach beyond geographic limitations to attract more students.

However, it became apparent that putting classes online was not simple. As those in the institutions who advocated online learning found out, educating people on a computer instead of in a classroom demands more from faculty members and administrators than just posting lessons and answering e-mails. Faculty members report that teaching students via the Internet is much more challenging and time consuming than teaching face-to-face. Many institutions providing online courses have become knowledgeable and sophisticated about what works and what doesn't. Online providers are finding out what distance students want and need and are changing their methods of designing and implementing courses. With the increase in providers, the competition for students is greater. No doubt you have come across ads for online learning on various Web sites.

· ·

"The Digital Natives, Gen Xers, and the Net Generation students in the classroom will push online learning and force us to do a better job. They won't be tolerant of text-based learning. They will want highly interactive classes. Gen Xers like online education, but the NetGen demands it."

Carol Scarafiotti
Executive Consultant, Online Learning
Vice President Emeritus
Rio Salado College

· ·

Online learning has since spread into all levels of education—from kindergarten to postdoctoral degrees. Learners in remote areas can access a quality education, conduct research in digital libraries, and talk to fellow classmates no matter where they are located. Corporations have snapped up online training because it is more cost-effective. High school students can take advanced classes from colleges and universities that offer subjects to fit their needs, rather than depending on the accessibility of a nearby institution. Faculty members do not have to be "on campus" but can teach from anywhere. Thus students can learn from experts worldwide.

Not too long ago, online learning was an oddity. But it has become more and more the norm. Teachers in traditional classes regularly use Web-based elements of online learning. For instance, class schedules and course outlines for face-to-face students are posted online, as are PowerPoint™ lecture notes for review.

IT'S GETTING BETTER ALL THE TIME

Technology Continues to Create Changes in Online Learning

Online course developers today regularly use VoIP, Webcasts, PowerPoint, videos, graphics, and animation. Some speculate that holograms and interactive games will soon become part of the mix. The commercial technology that allows people to digitally record TV programs is propelling academia into using more leading-edge technology. The buzz is that portable devices are the next generation of tools for online educators. In addition, handheld

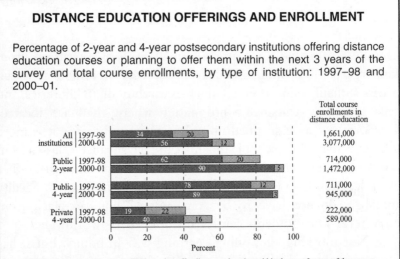

DISTANCE EDUCATION OFFERINGS AND ENROLLMENT

Percentage of 2-year and 4-year postsecondary institutions offering distance education courses or planning to offer them within the next 3 years of the survey and total course enrollments, by type of institution: 1997–98 and 2000–01.

SOURCE: Lewis, L., Snow, K., Farris, E., and Levin, D. (1999). *Distance Education at Postsecondary Education Institutions: 1997–98* (NCES 2000–013), tables 2 and 5; and Waits, T., and Lewis, L. (2003). *Distance Education at Degree-Granting Postsecondary Institutions: 2000–2001* (NCES 2003–017), tables 1 and 4. Data from U.S. Department of Education, NCES, Postsecondary Education Quick Information System (PEQIS), "Survey on Distance Education at Postsecondary Education Institutions," 1997–98 and "Survey on Distance Education at Higher Education Institutions," 2000–2001.

devices, such as cell phones, cameras, and digital music players, multiply the options for how people will interact in online courses. Online educators are exploring the use of computer simulation so that students can work together on projects. Imagine yourself as a medical student working on a computer-simulated operation or an engineering student building a manufacturing system. Even video games, with their levels of difficulty and multiple situations and characters, are possibilities for online course developers.

Bandwidth is the bottleneck for all these changes. As soon as people can quickly and cost-effectively download complex software, more and more advanced technologies will be introduced into online learning programs. Those who are designing the methods to deliver online courses assume that in a few years most students will have high-speed, less expensive Internet connections. This will allow them to use the "gee whiz" technology that is constantly emerging.

• •

"We are only in the beginning stages of what is possible. Our daily experience with online tools is so pervasive that our expectations are changing."

Mark David Milliron, Ph.D.
Vice President, Education Practice
SAS Institute, Inc.

• •

The Enormous Variety of Online Classes Will Only Grow Larger

You might assume that subjects such as graphic arts and languages aren't offered online, but they are. And although classes in forensics or grading diamonds are not as prevalent as business economics, even they are out there for you! A. Frank Mayadas, Ph.D., Program Director at the Alfred P. Sloan Foundation, predicts that the breadth of online classes will widen tremendously. He recalls talking to a man who wanted to teach a course at a traditional university on the second movements of Mozart symphonies but couldn't find enough students to enroll in it. However, Mayadas surmises that if the class were offered online, there would be interested students from all over the world. His is not such an outrageous prediction. The scope of online classes offered is stunning and getting more so.

· ·

"At some point, we will see courses available online that are not available on campus. The reason is that today if institutions offer specialized courses, they might not get enough students on campus to attend them. But on the Web, they can."

A. Frank Mayadas, Ph.D.
Program Director
Alfred P. Sloan Foundation

· ·

Simultaneous Enrollment at Several Educational Institutions Will Be Widespread

The development of a multi-institutional curriculum is expected in online education. For instance, a student getting a degree in art history from one institution wants to enroll in a course on art appraisal, but her institution doesn't offer it. So she signs up at another university that has an agreement with her home institution to transfer credits.

Increasingly, institutions are collaborating to design and deliver curricula by drawing from the best minds and experiences each offers. Students enrolled at one of the institutions in the group could take courses at any of the other institutions.

The Digital Divide Will Narrow

The digital divide keeps some segments of the population from taking advantage of online education. High-speed Internet connections aren't available to some groups of people because of cost or location. With the help of a National Science Foundation grant, the American Distance Education Consortium is researching how to get remote American Indian Tribal Colleges, Historically Black Colleges and Universities, and institutions with high Hispanic enrollment linked up to advanced Internet-satellite technology, which provides faster and cheaper connections.

. . . .

"You can typically get Internet connections four or five different ways in urban areas. In poor and rural areas, you take what you get. . . . Increasingly, you can put technology anywhere if you have the money. Poor people are still at the edges of the network."

Janet Poley, Ph.D.
President
American Distance Education Consortium

. . . .

Who and What Make Online Learning Hot?

Easy answer: It's convenient and engaging, and a lot of people want to participate. If you can find your way around a computer well enough to send and receive e-mails and get on the Internet, you are a potential online learner. Online learning allows you to pursue degrees, certificates, and professional training or take courses and just-plain-fun classes on a computer at times that fit your schedule. You don't have to commute to a campus, find parking, and show up at a certain hour for class. Plus, the technical demands of online learning are not that tricky. In just a few years, several developments have converged to cause a remarkable surge in online learning programs.

YOU DRIVE THE ONLINE LEARNING DEMAND

Online learners are a diverse bunch in age, occupation, background, geographic location, interest, and computer proficiency. They range from the kindergarten child playing learning games on the computer to the octogenarian taking a course in financial management. The high school student who wants to learn about Greek sculpture can do so for credit. Single parents can fit studying, writing papers, and taking tests into their chaotic schedules. Online technology opens doors for those who couldn't have gotten an education in the past. In 2003, more than 1.9 million students took classes online. That number was expected to grow to 2.6 million by the fall of 2004, as predicted by the Alfred P. Sloan Foundation, an organization that surveys distance education, in their report, *Entering the Mainstream: The Quality and Extent of Online Education in the United States, 2003 and 2004.*

You Are a Working Adult

When online learning came on the scene, it was primarily geared for adults in their late twenties to mid-thirties who were working and wanted to either get or complete a bachelor's degree or continue their education with a master's or other training. In the past, taking evening courses was about the only way to get that education. Online learning has made a huge difference. Some online adult learners take courses to finish up degrees they started but never completed. Others plug holes in their resumes. Others take advantage of employer-funded education.

Teacher Feedback | Student Story | Student Feedback

Full-time employee, wife, mother, and online learner

Gwen Washington never thought she could go back to school, as she was raising three children and working full-time. Online education gave her the chance. She earned her B.S. in legal studies and is now on her way to earning her M.B.A. "I've worked in the secretarial field all my life and don't have the experience to offer an employer more than what I do now. My education is the bridge to where I want to go," she says. Time was the biggest challenge for her with three children at home. But she made the decision to get the education she so dearly wanted by asking herself, "If not now, when?" Her determination gave her the ability to read on the train while commuting to her job and skip lunch with friends to do homework. "There is no reason why anyone who wants a degree can't get it, although," she adds, "I won't say it's easy."

You Are Working After Graduating from High School

Today's job market requires the skills of college graduates, yet research from the Bureau of Labor Statistics indicates that more students coming out of high school must work. As of May 2005,

93.2 percent of high school graduates enrolled in college were full-time and of these, 42.1 percent were employed or had looked for work the previous fall. Of the college students enrolled part-time, 82.4 percent were working.

Online learning is a boon for high school graduates who think that college is out of reach because they must work. Campus-based classes are usually scheduled during working hours. Yes, you could attend evening classes, but what if there is no college or community college nearby? Those who are enrolled in college and must juggle class times with work or take fewer classes benefit from online courses.

. . . .

"We are rapidly moving into an era where knowledge, education, and training count far more if you are going to be player on any level of the economic ladder. For any rung, you have to be trained. At the higher end, you have to be educated. Although there is far greater need, people have far less time."

A. Frank Mayadas, Ph.D.
Program Director
Alfred P. Sloan Foundation

. . . .

You Are Retired, but Your Mind Isn't

For many, retirement means having the time to play golf or take up scrapbooking. The 22 percent of people over 65 who use the Internet, according to a Pew Internet and American Life Project, *Older Americans and the Internet*, are just as likely to take an online course about something that interests them. They could even be professionals reaching the age where they can collect Social Security but instead start second, third, or fourth careers.

Increasingly, retirees want to be active and so head back to college. Online learning allows them to participate without sitting in a classroom.

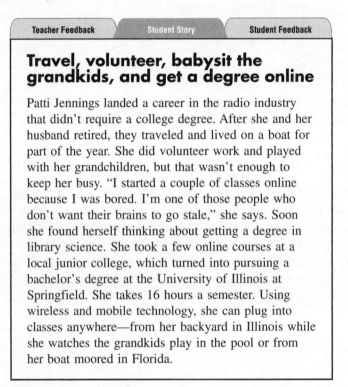

| Teacher Feedback | Student Story | Student Feedback |

Travel, volunteer, babysit the grandkids, and get a degree online

Patti Jennings landed a career in the radio industry that didn't require a college degree. After she and her husband retired, they traveled and lived on a boat for part of the year. She did volunteer work and played with her grandchildren, but that wasn't enough to keep her busy. "I started a couple of classes online because I was bored. I'm one of those people who don't want their brains to go stale," she says. Soon she found herself thinking about getting a degree in library science. She took a few online courses at a local junior college, which turned into pursuing a bachelor's degree at the University of Illinois at Springfield. She takes 16 hours a semester. Using wireless and mobile technology, she can plug into classes anywhere—from her backyard in Illinois while she watches the grandkids play in the pool or from her boat moored in Florida.

You Are in the Military

All the services encourage members to continue their education, whether that means finishing high school, taking college-level courses, or earning a degree. Many institutions of higher education offering online courses have agreements to provide education to military service people, and many military installations have learning centers with computer access and cyber cafes and libraries with computer linkups. The only caveat is that the service member's chosen institution must be regionally accredited.

For example, the eArmyU offers 146 programs from twenty-nine different colleges and universities. Soldiers can earn anything from a certificate to an associate, bachelor's, or master's degree through Web-based courses. Members of the Air Force can take academic or technical courses from two- or four-year institutions on base, off base, or by correspondence. The Navy has partnerships with colleges and universities that offer rating-related degrees via distance learning. Sailors can earn an associate degree in oceanography technology or a bachelor's degree in management of technical operations. Marines can take any kind of course for any kind of degree on campus, online, or via correspondence.

You Have a Disability

According to the National Center for Education Statistics, 20 percent of the undergraduates enrolled in the United States have some form of disability. Jeff Ian Finlay, then assistant director at the Center for Media and New Technologies at the University of Maryland University College, recalls speaking with a blind student who said his experience with distance education two decades before had been disastrous—textbooks sent in the mail didn't arrive on time or weren't in Braille. But now the adaptive technology, screen-reader software, and equipment he has at his disposal in his workplace enable him to take online courses much more easily.

Services at online institutions vary widely as accommodations available to online students evolve. Says Finlay, "It hasn't come to the fore as a major issue in online education. It's a matter of collaboration between the people responsible for technology and disability support services."

. . . .

"I have a good example of the power of online learning for people with disabilities. A professor of ours was looking at the discussion board for a course on bilingual education that was almost finished. A student in the class posted a message saying, 'I've been meaning to tell you that I'm deaf. When I got into this class, I realized no one knew. This is the first time in my life that I wasn't different.'"

Lori McNabb
Manager
Student and Faculty Services
University of Texas System TeleCampus

. . . .

Teacher Feedback	Student Story	Student Feedback

Hearing impaired and an online learner

Bill Glenn tried to attend regular classes a few times but his hearing disability made it too difficult. His wife began researching online learning for herself and, as Glenn puts it, "I just sort of followed her right into it." He is getting his associate degree in information technology at Kaplan University while working full-time. He hasn't had to ask for assistance because of his hearing impairment since most of the information he needs for the class is text-based. Occasionally, though, his class does have an audio section. When that happens, he wears a headset over his hearing aids and manipulates it so that he can hear. "I've enjoyed the distance learning so far," he says, "and I can actually get the degree that I've sought for a long time."

MILES OR MINUTES FROM THE CLASSROOM—IT DOESN'T MATTER

Online students are located in just about every part of the world. All you need is an Internet connection. Ray Schroeder, Professor Emeritus, Faculty Associate, and Director of Technology-Enhanced Learning at the University of Illinois at Springfield, where online students have enrolled from five continents and thirty-nine states, recalls that recently one student was deployed in Iraq and one was living on a sailboat in Kodiak, Alaska, heading for Chile. You can't get much more geographically different than that.

But you don't have to live on the outskirts to be an online learner. Full-time on-campus students take online courses at their universities to resolve scheduling conflicts or pick up extra classes they need. Students augment their studies and earn better grades by reviewing the lecture they heard in class a day ago or looking at the teacher's PowerPoint notes. If they miss class, they can easily read the lecture.

In addition, institutions of higher education are "blending" classes that are held in physical classrooms in campus buildings by conducting part of the class online at other times during the week. In some classes, students can choose to either come to class or participate via their computers.

LIFELONG LEARNING

The days are over when you got your college degree and that was enough education to last your lifetime. Continuous learning is a necessity for those who must keep up with rapidly changing skill levels and the escalating amount of knowledge needed in the workplace. The Bureau of Education states that in 2002–03, 40 percent of adults who were 16 and above participated in adult education for work-related reasons.

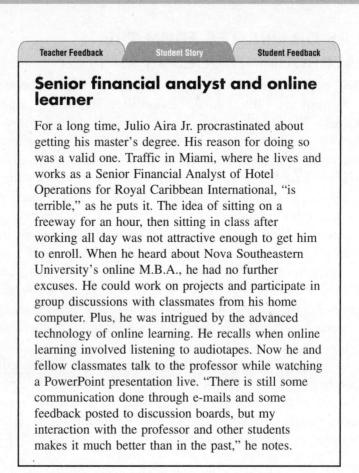

Teacher Feedback | Student Story | Student Feedback

Senior financial analyst and online learner

For a long time, Julio Aira Jr. procrastinated about getting his master's degree. His reason for doing so was a valid one. Traffic in Miami, where he lives and works as a Senior Financial Analyst of Hotel Operations for Royal Caribbean International, "is terrible," as he puts it. The idea of sitting on a freeway for an hour, then sitting in class after working all day was not attractive enough to get him to enroll. When he heard about Nova Southeastern University's online M.B.A., he had no further excuses. He could work on projects and participate in group discussions with classmates from his home computer. Plus, he was intrigued by the advanced technology of online learning. He recalls when online learning involved listening to audiotapes. Now he and fellow classmates talk to the professor while watching a PowerPoint presentation live. "There is still some communication done through e-mails and some feedback posted to discussion boards, but my interaction with the professor and other students makes it much better than in the past," he notes.

. . . .

"The shelf life of a college education these days has been reduced to no more than three or four years. Most of us will have to 'go to school' for the rest of our working lives just to keep pace in a globally competitive workplace. Plus, most of us will face at least five or six significant job changes in our careers. There are few better or more practical options for you to keep learning than distance education. Given the nature of the information age, the ever-increasing demands for workplace 'up-skilling,' and the increasing mobility of our society, just about everyone will become a distance learning student in the twenty-first century."

Michael P. Lambert
Executive Director
The Distance Education and Training Council

. . . .

ACCEPTANCE OF ONLINE DEGREES GROWS

Employers want to know if future employees have the skills to do the job, not if they received their education online. Vicky Phillips, CEO of GetEducated.com, regularly conducts surveys on online learning. Starting in 1989, GetEducated.com began surveying corporate employers to ascertain their attitudes toward online students. She found that since the Internet emerged as a vehicle for distance learning, their acceptance of online students has gone way up.

In the 2000 survey, 79 percent of the respondents rated online education as good as residential, whereas only 50 percent thought it was as good in 1989. She reasons that the Internet has a lot to do with the higher approval ratings. Another factor is name recognition. More than 90 percent of corporate employers approved of online learning if they knew about the college or university, even if it was a small local college. Large public university systems fared much better. As Phillips notes, "They are pulling from a brick and mortar legacy."

Companies today value the skills that students get from learning online—being able to work with teams on the Internet and experience in collaborating with people from other countries and cultures. Online students are used to contributing ideas, leading virtual teams, and following leaders who are not sitting across from them in a conference room. Online education is becoming internationalized with partnerships between institutions of higher education across oceans and continents. Virginia Tech, for instance, has an exchange between undergraduate students in Belgium and another with the University of Saudi Arabia. One of Virginia Tech's engineering classes collaborates with students in Germany to design cars.

TECHNOLOGY IS INCREASINGLY COST-EFFECTIVE

Googling is a verb. People already haggle over used cars on the Internet. Kids look up phone numbers online and grandmothers check their bank accounts. And if you're a NetGen or Millennial, the Internet is something you grew up with. What's a typewriter? Older students want online courses out of necessity. Having grown up with computers, the next generation takes online courses because they like being online.

Chapter 2: Who and What Make Online Learning Hot?

Teacher Feedback	Student Story	Student Feedback

I used VoIP in a class I took. I would log in to a virtual classroom and could hear the instructor and see what he was typing on his computer. He could see who else was logged in so he knew who was there. We were able to have conversations between a guy from Japan and someone from Canada and three other local people. There is no limit to the number of people you can have online. All you need is a computer that has a speaker and a microphone.

Pami Ahluwalia
Master's Student
Computer Information Systems
University of Denver, University College

As technology becomes more user-friendly, the possibilities of accomplishing more complex tasks become less intimidating. Internet connections get faster so that online students don't have to wait a half hour for a graphic or video to download. Software is continuously updated and good quality hard drives get cheaper. Distance learning providers can cost-effectively provide the services that support online students, such as virtual libraries and online student advisers. Not only are up-and-coming online learners familiar with the latest gizmos, they also force online education providers to come up to *their* speed.

Though the technology requirements for online learning aren't difficult, signing up for your first online class can be intimidating. High-quality online providers offer help via online tutorials or CDs in how to use and install the software needed to take the course. Students get help from mentors who walk them through the process by phone or e-mail.

· ·

"At some point, online technology will become just another tool in education. We no longer talk about the utility of the telephone. It's now part of the background. As bandwidth increases, we will be able to do more and more."

Gerald Heeger
President
University of Maryland University College

· ·

▶ TECHNICAL TERMINOLOGY

Not every online education provider is at technology's cutting edge, so you might not run into everything on the following list. However, you should have a sense of the technology that is either currently in use or is on an online learning provider's wish list. Though most students will have few problems using these technologies, it's wise to be in close contact with the tech-support people when you first begin an online program to find out if and how your computer will support the necessary software.

Computer simulation Online students in science and business may find computer simulation in their classes. Simulations can range from graphics of interactive molecules in a biology class to a simulation of a case study in which students are asked to make business decisions.

Digital television You might confuse digital television with High Definition TV (HDTV), but it is really more akin to *video streaming* and is very common in online learning programs. With digital television, you can receive more channels without using more bandwidth. Digital television works best with a broadband Internet connection.

Graphical User Interface (GUI) A complicated name for the technology that gives you graphic symbols and icons and allows you to use a mouse to access your computer's operating system.

Interactive TV Many cable television providers provide interactive television in the form of "video on demand," so you may already be using this technology. The potential for this technology in online learning is enormous. For instance, online providers, in conjunction with a cable company, could offer a series of lectures for viewers to access on demand.

Podcast This technology allows audio files to be delivered online. For instance, online teachers can record monthly lectures as an MP3 and distribute them to students, who can then choose when to listen.

PowerPoint This graphic presentation technology is commonly used in classrooms and corporations. A number of companies take the technology and combine it with audio narration. For use in online learning, it is compressed into a Web-friendly file that can easily be downloaded.

Push technology Another name for this technology is Really Simple Syndication (RSS). It is commonly used to get a constant feed of current events or information from specific servers. In online learning, teachers use it to send students announcements, reminders, and monthly lecture series.

Real-time audio/real-time video You will find a number of products that enable you to be involved in a class with the teacher and other students via audio or video in real time. This might include a whiteboard appearing on your monitor on which you, the teacher, and other students interact.

Streaming audio/streaming video Audio or video begins playing as soon as it is received by your PC, instead of waiting until the entire file is downloaded.

Videoconferencing Used mostly over the Internet, this technology allows students at remote sites to connect to a class using their PC and a broadband Internet connection. They can see what a camera sees in the classroom, as well as hear and interact with other students and the teacher.

Virtual laboratories You might want to sign up for a biology lab just for the fun of virtually dissecting a virtual frog. But online computer classes also use virtual laboratories so that teachers can demonstrate what they're lecturing about and students can work on problems.

Voice Over Internet Protocol (VoIP) Using a microphone and speakers or headphone, online students can have voice conversations over the computer with other students and the teacher.

Web conferencing Teachers and students use audio, video, and interactive whiteboards to communicate during mostly synchronous classes.

Web whiteboarding Teachers draw or write on a whiteboard and students can instantly see the material. Students can also use the whiteboard by drawing on the monitor with either a stylus or mouse.

(Note: This list was written with the help of Dr. Theodore Stone, Acting Associate Provost, Instructional Services and Support, University of Maryland University College.)

CHAPTER 3

But Wait—There's More!

While online learning is big in distance education, don't forget there are other ways people learn at a distance and have done so for years. To be sure, online learning will continue to proliferate and improve technically but not everyone has access to high-speed Internet connections or even access to a computer for that matter. Some people do prefer learning from correspondence courses or gathering with other students to watch videotaped lectures.

CORRESPONDENCE COURSES—EDUCATION AT YOUR OWN PACE

For many, correspondence courses are still the best way to take a course or complete a degree. For people without Internet access, such as prison inmates and students in remote international locations, correspondence courses may be the only way. Correspondence and independent learning courses are also typically cheaper than online courses—another reason for their continuation.

While correspondence courses generally allow students to enroll at any time, they usually must complete the course within a certain specified period. Not too long ago students in correspondence courses had up to a year; however, educational institutions are beginning to shorten time limits to six or eight months. At Penn State World Campus, which has provided correspondence and independent learning courses since 1892, students take "paced" correspondence-type courses, which start and end in a semester time frame. Interestingly, students in paced courses often have a significantly higher completion rate than those who have six to eight months to finish a course.

Teacher Feedback | Student Story | Student Feedback

Here's the syllabus, here's the book, here are the assignments— now it's up to you

While Terri Burris was working at Virginia Tech, she took a few graduate classes on campus toward her master's in education. But then along came a required class that unfortunately was scheduled for 2 o'clock in the afternoon. She immediately signed up for VTOnline, Virginia Tech's e-Learning program, and kept right on going, even after she left Virginia Tech to start a new job as Director of Annual and Leadership Giving at the University of North Carolina at Greensboro.

Because she is a super-organized person, Burris likes getting the entire lineup of each class for the semester so she can work ahead. A few weeks before the semester ends, Burris is already kicking back. She gets the reading list, the syllabus, and assignments from her teacher. She notes deadlines for assignments and papers and immediately starts the course work. There is not much interaction between her and her teacher, but she doesn't mind studying this way, although she does miss hearing a professor's point of view. Some classes take 2 hours a week and others take 4 or more hours per week per class. One to two nights a week she stays after work to do the reading and writing, as she finds there are fewer distractions in her quiet office. Though she's getting her master's completely online, she feels that some portion of an undergraduate and graduate class should be in a real classroom. "I know that for people doing research in the medical or nursing fields there is a lot of interaction with professors or advisers. My degree requirements are more focused on studying and reading," she says.

. . . .

"We serve a different niche of learners. Learners who want to work independently, one on one with their instructor, and proceed through a course at their own pace, elect independent learning courses over paced and online courses."

Peter A. Rubba, Ed.D.
Senior Director
Penn State World Campus

. . . .

OFF-SITE LEARNING VIA REAL-TIME VIDEOCONFERENCING

Site-based distance learning that takes place in classrooms away from the main campus of an educational institution is still very much in use. Students attend classes in locations such as office complexes or hotel conference rooms and receive instruction from either videotapes of lectures or real-time, online videos of live lectures. In the former, students only can observe and listen. In the latter, students are active participants.

Teacher Feedback   Student Story   Student Feedback

His professor is on TV and so is he

About three quarters of the way through his M.B.A. from the Institute for Distance and Distributed Learning at Virginia Polytechnic Institute, Steve Yob has taken some classes online and some by videoconferencing. Even though he meets in a classroom in an office building with other students for a 4-hour class once a week, he definitely likes the videoconferencing, or Vtel, much better than the purely online classes he's taken. Though their professor is live at a videoconferencing studio in Virginia, Yob and his fellow students see the professor, and he them, just as if they were all in the same classroom. When students want to ask a question, they press a button on a microphone and the camera zooms in. Students see any diagrams or illustrations the professor wants to include.

DISTRIBUTED LEARNING: WHEN THE TEACHER COMES TO THE STUDENTS

Distributed learning, or distributed education, is yet another form of distance education that has been in use for some time. Rather than moving people to the classroom, professors come to their students. Students in distributed education classes generally enroll in cohorts and progress through the course together. This form of distance education is used quite often for M.B.A. programs. For instance, students in Nova Southeastern University's M.B.A. program meet in 13-hour increments for five weekends, starting Friday night and continuing all day Saturday. Says Preston Jones, Ph.D., Associate Dean of Academic Affairs at Nova Southeastern University, "We have found that adult learners don't need as much time in classes." Adjunct and full-time professors fly from Nova's Fort Lauderdale location or other locations to off-site locations. Students are expected to meet during the week to work on group projects.

Teacher Feedback | Student Story | Student Feedback

My professor flies in for our weekly classes

Friday evenings from 6 p.m. to 10 p.m. and Saturdays from 8 a.m. to 5 p.m., John Bohn sits with fifteen other students in front of a professor who routinely flies in each week to teach the class. In about a year, Bohn will get his degree from Nova Southeastern University. But for now he's quite satisfied to learn from professors who, he says, have extensive global experience. He explains that he likes the fact that they have years of hands-on experience in private industry, are application oriented, and aren't "professors who just sit in an office and only publish."

The 18-month fast-track M.B.A. program is demanding, but Bohn likes the class exercises, case studies, and discussions they have almost every session. "The professor divvies us up into small groups and we discuss issues or case studies. We take turns picking a committee chairman. Then we present our findings to the class," he comments. Though there is plenty of face-to-face interaction, Bohn does lots of writing in response to the questions the professor throws out weekly. During the week, Bohn researches and reads articles, then writes an essay that he'll post online for comments from other classmates. He is expected to comment on two or three of the other essays posted that week. As he finishes up the degree, Bohn must travel to Fort Lauderdale, where Nova Southeastern is located, for a one-week capstone program.

He likes the camaraderie with the others. "It's a close-knit group," he explains. "We sometimes go out to dinner with the instructors."

. . . .

"The founder of Nova Southeastern University described the classroom as being comprised of faculty and students. When people can't leave their jobs, we make it convenient for them by flying professors to meet with them and learning takes place. We have adjunct and full-time professors. We also have administrators so that students receive customer service."

Preston Jones, Ph.D.
Associate Dean, Academic Affairs
Nova Southeastern University

. . . .

BLENDED OR HYBRID LEARNING: LEARNING ONLINE AND FACE-TO-FACE

When traditional institutions of higher education first provided classes over the Internet, the chasm between face-to-face and online learning was wide. But that didn't last for long. As students and teachers began to recognize the advantages of online learning, elements of online teaching started popping up in face-to-face classes. Teachers posted lecture notes and class schedules on class Web sites. On-campus students who worked part time or who needed a certain class that conflicted with their schedules realized they could take classes online. Institutions offering face-to-face classes, coupled with a few online courses for students living far away, were amazed to find that many of their on-campus students were taking the online classes, too.

The buzz started—online learning gave students the ability to squeeze in a few classes they wouldn't have ordinarily been able to take. Students who worked during the day at part-time jobs were no longer limited in which classes they could take. Blended learning took off and has become a staple in higher education. "I don't envision online learning replacing face-to-face learning," says Mark Kretovics, Ph.D., Assistant Professor of Higher Education Administration at Kent State University, "but it's a great complement. Every class that I teach is Web-supported."

Teachers found that when there are more online components to their face-to-face classes, students learn better and retain more because they can access the class materials in additional ways. In traditional face-to-face classes, students take copious notes and then have background materials to read in a textbook or resource in the library. However, if those elements can be supplemented by video and audio modules, learning takes place in a variety of ways.

When it became evident that online learning was viable and effective and enhanced face-to-face learning, teachers of on-campus students began scheduling classes that met both in the classroom and online. Now, some meet mostly online and get together in the classroom before midterms and finals. Hybrid classes include putting lectures online and then holding small face-to-face classes so students can interact with each other on projects and assignments. In other types of blends, online students meet face-to-face for a few weekends a semester. The University of Illinois at Springfield, for instance, offers online certification programs in mathematics. A portion of the course is held in face-to-face classes that occur two to three weekends a semester, while the remainder of the course is online.

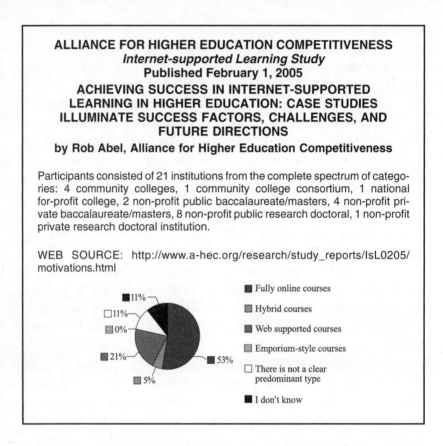

ALLIANCE FOR HIGHER EDUCATION COMPETITIVENESS
Internet-supported Learning Study
Published February 1, 2005
ACHIEVING SUCCESS IN INTERNET-SUPPORTED LEARNING IN HIGHER EDUCATION: CASE STUDIES ILLUMINATE SUCCESS FACTORS, CHALLENGES, AND FUTURE DIRECTIONS
by Rob Abel, Alliance for Higher Education Competitiveness

Participants consisted of 21 institutions from the complete spectrum of categories: 4 community colleges, 1 community college consortium, 1 national for-profit college, 2 non-profit public baccalaureate/masters, 4 non-profit private baccalaureate/masters, 8 non-profit public research doctoral, 1 non-profit private research doctoral institution.

WEB SOURCE: http://www.a-hec.org/research/study_reports/IsL0205/motivations.html

- 11%
- 11%
- 0%
- 21%
- 5%
- 53%

- ■ Fully online courses
- ▥ Hybrid courses
- ▤ Web supported courses
- ▤ Emporium-style courses
- □ There is not a clear predominant type
- ■ I don't know

"Blends will revolutionize education in urban classes," remarks A. Frank Mayadas, Ph.D., Program Director of the Sloan Foundation, noting that in rural areas students still must drive to a class on campus. He surmises that in ten years there will be few face-to-face classes without any elements of Web-supported materials or learning.

Even with all the enthusiasm about blended learning, Melody Thompson, D.Ed., Director of the American Center for the Study of Distance Education and the Director of Planning and Research at Pennsylvania State University's Continuing Education, has a few reservations about focusing entirely on blended classes. While she is all for the capability of augmenting traditional education with online learning and limiting the times students meet in classes, she thinks purely online and purely face-to-face will always be needed. "Some people cannot come to campus at all. We had one student in Antarctica, for instance. Because of the history of distance education as a movement to provide access to people, I would hate to think that the focus would be solely on blended learning. People recognize that face-to-face has its own unique benefits, too," she comments.

• •

"I tried teaching a blended learning class. It met 3 hours at a time every other week. If students missed the classroom class, they were gone from the rest of the students for nearly a month. I would forget who they were. I want to know that student who comes in to my class and refers to what they wrote last week. There weren't enough face-to-face meetings to get to know them well enough."

Susan G. Sharpe
English Professor
Northern Virginia Community College

• •

▶Part II

WHAT Are My Options?

Search

Chapter 4 `Go`

From Associate Degrees to Graduate Degrees

What if you are interested in learning about forensics or want to take a creative writing class for credit toward a bachelor's degree? These—and thousands more courses that one wouldn't ordinarily think could be taught via the Internet—are available online.

A. Frank Mayadas, Ph.D., Program Director of the Sloan Foundation, observes that asynchronous learning will drive online learning to provide classes on a breadth and scale hardly imaginable. He sees specialized courses growing and notes that it's already happening. Online learners now have a spectacular range of possibilities, from full-fledged doctorates to classes in doll-making.

When distance learning was first developing, it was primarily geared toward working adults in their late twenties to mid-thirties. They wanted to enhance their career development or get the degree they hadn't gotten because of jobs and families. Institutions that offered online learning catered to their interests, with professional courses and degrees in business and health. Now, as the technology used to deliver online learning becomes more advanced and online learning is more accepted, the subject matter of courses is becoming more diverse. For instance, younger students who want to get a liberal arts bachelor's degree online need more options. "Online learning is still very much in the career area," says Brian Mueller, CEO of the University of Phoenix Online. But he surmises that as younger students get involved in online learning, they will want to have more liberal arts courses leading to degrees simply because they are used to an online environment and for the convenience it gives them.

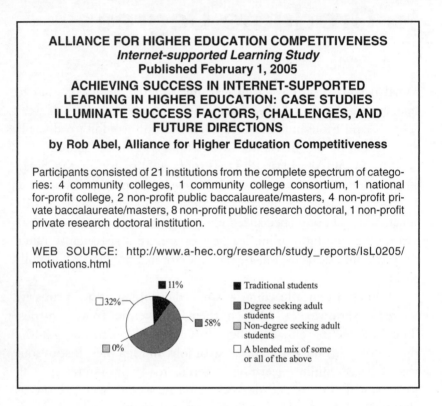

ALLIANCE FOR HIGHER EDUCATION COMPETITIVENESS
Internet-supported Learning Study
Published February 1, 2005
ACHIEVING SUCCESS IN INTERNET-SUPPORTED LEARNING IN HIGHER EDUCATION: CASE STUDIES ILLUMINATE SUCCESS FACTORS, CHALLENGES, AND FUTURE DIRECTIONS
by Rob Abel, Alliance for Higher Education Competitiveness

Participants consisted of 21 institutions from the complete spectrum of categories: 4 community colleges, 1 community college consortium, 1 national for-profit college, 2 non-profit public baccalaureate/masters, 4 non-profit private baccalaureate/masters, 8 non-profit public research doctoral, 1 non-profit private research doctoral institution.

WEB SOURCE: http://www.a-hec.org/research/study_reports/IsL0205/motivations.html

- 11% ■ Traditional students
- 32% ■ Degree seeking adult students
- 58% ■ Non-degree seeking adult students
- 0% □ A blended mix of some or all of the above

DO YOU WANT TRAINING OR EDUCATION?

Your choice of online institution will be greatly affected by your need for either training or education. Training focuses on increasing a skill or knowledge specific to a profession or job. Education is more theoretical and designed to develop broad knowledge. Online learners who want to earn academic credit toward a degree won't have the same criteria as someone looking for a specific skill. Mueller contends that younger students want more of a theoretical education, but the 35-five-year-old wants a blend of the practical and the theoretical. It's the difference between going through the full admissions process, showing your transcripts, and receiving a grade and credit toward a degree and taking a course and getting a certificate that will not carry any credit.

ASSOCIATE DEGREES

The two most common associate degrees are the Associate of Arts (A.A.) and the Associate of Science (A.S.), with others such as the Associate of Business Administration (A.B.A.) and the Associate of General Studies (A.G.S.). Usually students in associate degree programs take two years to finish. But if they are part-time, it can take a lot longer to earn the 60 to 64 credits required.

The growth of online courses in community colleges has been extremely rapid, fueled in part because so many people who want a college degree work, have families, or lack the funds to take off four years to go to a traditional college. From her observations about enrollment at Rio Salado College, Carol Scarafiotti, Executive Consultant, Online Learning, Vice President Emeritus, observes that online learning for students getting an associate degree is catching on. Rio Salado College had about 6,000 students in their online courses in 1996. By the spring of 2005, 24,000 students were enrolled.

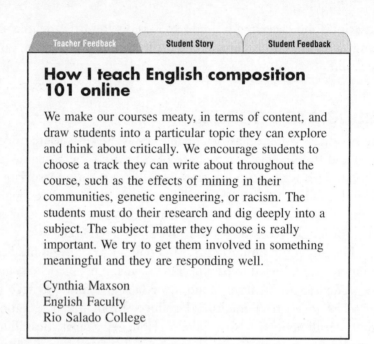

How I teach English composition 101 online

We make our courses meaty, in terms of content, and draw students into a particular topic they can explore and think about critically. We encourage students to choose a track they can write about throughout the course, such as the effects of mining in their communities, genetic engineering, or racism. The students must do their research and dig deeply into a subject. The subject matter they choose is really important. We try to get them involved in something meaningful and they are responding well.

Cynthia Maxson
English Faculty
Rio Salado College

BACHELOR'S DEGREES

Generally, the bachelor's degree is recognized worldwide as the first university degree you earn. Although students enrolled full-time can earn the degree in four years, many take up to six years to earn the required 120 to 128 credits.

In most colleges and universities, the course of study that leads to a bachelor's degree consists of concentrated work in a major, such as psychology or business, and wide-ranging work in a variety of subjects, such as the liberal arts, to give students a broad foundation of knowledge. However, some bachelor's degree programs focus on intensive study in a particular field without the broad liberal arts background. The most common bachelor's degrees are the Bachelor of Arts (B.A.) and the Bachelor of Science (B.S.), although there are many other titles.

It used to be that if you were getting a bachelor's degree online you were probably in your mid-thirties, working, and had a family. Now the age of the typical undergraduate online student is dropping because many people have to work full-time and can't go to a traditional campus. According to the National Center for Education Statistics' *Education Statistics Quarterly*, 2004, approximately 57 percent of undergraduates taking postsecondary degrees from 1999–2000 were 23 years old or younger.

Teacher Feedback	Student Story	Student Feedback

How I teach my chemistry course online

We have a calendar that outlines what is going to be covered in each class and refers students to what chapters and sections of the textbooks will be covered that day. In my calendar I also include links to the outline of the material covered that day with keywords and explicit notes on the sections of the book discussed. We use Web-based homework (which I don't collect) that tells the students what is expected of them. The Web page provides all the details students need to get information on their own. Instructors in all the chemistry classes give the same exam, even though each instructor may cover a topic differently. We all have to be at the same place when an exam is given.

Jimmy Reeves, Ph.D.
Associate Professor, Chemistry
University of North Carolina at Wilmington

In the past, online providers discouraged newly graduated high school students from getting their bachelor's online. The prevailing opinion was that students in their late teens or early twenties didn't have the self-discipline and time-management skills to succeed as online learners. However, students in college began signing up for online classes anyway. They discovered that the convenience and flexibility of online learning were just too good to be missed. In addition, online learning was nothing new to younger students, who grew up with online games and instant messaging.

Online learning program providers noted the trend and began offering undergraduate degrees to all ages. For instance, the University of Phoenix Online has developed a bachelor's degree program specifically for incoming freshmen of any age—particularly for those just out of high school. The University of Maryland University College reports that from 1998 to 2004, the number of undergraduate students who were 25 years old or younger, which is considered traditional college age, grew from 29 to 45 percent. It is the fastest growing segment of their student body and is expected to increase.

Teacher Feedback | Student Story | Student Feedback

An online learning program specifically for freshmen

People think that incoming freshmen lack discipline, but our program [for freshmen] is very organized. Instructors take attendance. Students must participate certain days of the week, from both a quantitative and qualitative standpoint, which involves attendance and participation. During the week, the classes are asynchronous; however, the faculty member must be online from 4 p.m. to 8 p.m. Monday through Thursday and from 5 p.m. to 9 p.m. on Sundays. We think it's important not to put freshmen in large lecture halls of 300 to 400 to learn economics or political science. We have small electronic classrooms with lots of contact between instructors and students.

Brian Mueller
CEO
University of Phoenix Online

Teacher Feedback **Student Story** **Student Feedback**

Finished up her bachelor's and on to her master's

Amy Kavalewitz works full-time as an administrator of Student Organizations and Foreign Programs at the South Texas College of Law. She is also the single mother of a 6-year-old and, after five years, received her bachelor's degree in liberal arts with a major in organizational leadership from the University of Phoenix Online. She soon will start her master's in adult education. Having experienced both face-to-face and online learning, she thinks the latter is much more challenging. "Anyone who dismisses distance learning as inferior has clearly never attempted an online course," she says.

Online discussion groups give her the feeling of being in a classroom. Communication with the different teachers varies. Most times, her professors respond to her e-mails and take part in the discussions. "You do encounter a professor who seems to be 'on vacation' or have other things going on, so the response time is slower or even too late when it concerns a particular question or assignment." While very frustrating, she says these occurrences are rare.

GRADUATE DEGREES

Online learning program providers predominantly offer master's degrees. It makes sense. The students who need to keep up their skills in the workplace or need graduate degrees to move ahead in their professions are most likely to have jobs and families. Online learning is a great fit for their busy lifestyle.

The master's degree is the first academic or professional degree earned after the bachelor's degree. A traditional, full-time master's degree student may take a year or two to earn the required 30 credits. In some master's degree programs, students are simply expected to take advanced-level courses and perhaps pass a culminating exam. In others, original research and a thesis are required. Some online learning programs have a brief residency requirement. Students usually earn a Master of Arts (M.A.), a Master of Science (M.S.), or a Master of Business Administration (M.B.A.) degree. Many of the online master's degree programs are professional in nature.

. . . .

"You can get a master's degree in almost anything you want to study. The professional master's degrees are relatively easy to set up, as are associate degrees, which also have lots of offerings. Where you don't see as many offerings is in the bachelor's completion area. The reason for that is that the tools aren't as developed for lab classes."

Janet Poley, Ph.D.
President
American Distance Education Consortium

. . . .

Another type of master's degree that is offered via online learning is the interdisciplinary degree, which offers students the option of designing their own course of study based on their particular interests. Some are offered in liberal studies or humanities and are granted for advanced study and a culminating project or thesis. Others combine academic and professional areas of study. For instance, students with interests in psychology and sociology can combine the two programs.

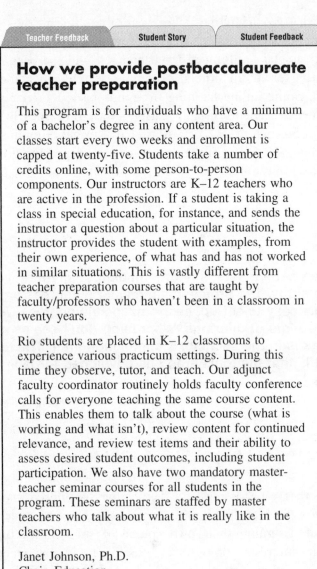

Teacher Feedback | Student Story | Student Feedback

How we provide postbaccalaureate teacher preparation

This program is for individuals who have a minimum of a bachelor's degree in any content area. Our classes start every two weeks and enrollment is capped at twenty-five. Students take a number of credits online, with some person-to-person components. Our instructors are K–12 teachers who are active in the profession. If a student is taking a class in special education, for instance, and sends the instructor a question about a particular situation, the instructor provides the student with examples, from their own experience, of what has and has not worked in similar situations. This is vastly different from teacher preparation courses that are taught by faculty/professors who haven't been in a classroom in twenty years.

Rio students are placed in K–12 classrooms to experience various practicum settings. During this time they observe, tutor, and teach. Our adjunct faculty coordinator routinely holds faculty conference calls for everyone teaching the same course content. This enables them to talk about the course (what is working and what isn't), review content for continued relevance, and review test items and their ability to assess desired student outcomes, including student participation. We also have two mandatory master-teacher seminar courses for all students in the program. These seminars are staffed by master teachers who talk about what it is really like in the classroom.

Janet Johnson, Ph.D.
Chair, Education
Rio Salado College

DOCTORAL DEGREES

The doctoral degree, the highest degree awarded, is earned after an advanced course of study that usually consists of original research, a dissertation, and extended written work. The traditional on-campus doctoral student takes four to ten years to complete the degree, but many distance learning doctoral programs are structured to streamline the process. The Doctor of Philosophy (Ph.D.) is the most common doctoral degree; it is awarded in fields that range from philosophy to geology. Other frequently awarded doctoral degrees include the Doctor of Education (Ed.D.), Doctor of Business Administration (D.B.A.), Doctor of Engineering (Eng.D.), and Doctor of Psychology (Psy.D.).

Not too long ago, if you wanted to get a doctoral degree online, you would have had a tough time finding one. There were far fewer online doctoral degree programs than master's degree programs. However, online doctoral courses are increasingly accepted. "It has spread like a good virus throughout education," says Michael P. Lambert, Executive Director of the Distance Education and Training Council. Lambert points out that it's not a stretch to earn a doctorate online, since doctoral students are already independent learners involved in independent research. He predicts that doctoral students will become much more common in ten years. Henry T. Radda, Ph.D., Director of the School for Advanced Studies at the University of Phoenix Online, comments that as perceptions about online education change, more potential doctoral candidates will consider getting their degree online. One of the advantages of online doctorates is that students are not just learning with and from people in their department, but with people from all over the world.

. . . .

"People are reluctant to earn doctoral degrees by the time they get to that point. They go to a university and are told they have to quit their jobs or work part-time. I had to do twenty weeks of residency and move my kids 90 miles from home. An online doctorate is not any easier, but it does allow the flexibility to have a life while earning the degree."

Dawn Iwamoto, Ed.D.
Dean, School for Advanced Studies
University of Phoenix Online

. . . .

Online doctoral programs are set up about the same as traditional departments. Students are expected to do concentrated independent research and critical thinking. They must work independently on a scholarly dissertation. At the University of Phoenix Online, candidates work with a mentor, chair, and committee members. Some courses are designed to be completely online, while others require a specific residency. In the third year, students must complete a collaborative case study that looks at real-world issues and scenarios with compounding problems. Teams switch between followers and leaders. Students must be in the online classroom five out of seven days and 15 to 20 hours a week, and they must attend three residencies in Phoenix.

From Certificates to Fun Classes

Since online learning has become so popular and accepted, the variety of classes available (in addition to undergraduate and graduate degrees) is astounding. Those who want to get certificates in just about any given subject will find more and more courses offered online. The Internet has brought a wealth of classes to the "casual" student who wants to learn, for example, to take better digital photos or fix car engines.

CERTIFICATE PROGRAMS

Certificate programs can be earned at the undergraduate or graduate level and usually consist of six to ten courses that are all focused on a single profession or subject. Some schools offer a portion of a master's or other degree as a certificate. This allows you to take part of the full degree curriculum and either stop at the certification level or proceed through and earn the entire degree. Either way, be sure to check admission requirements, as they may vary for earning a certificate versus earning a degree.

Professional Certificate Programs

Professional certificate programs are often designed with the help of professional associations and licensing boards and thus encompass real-world, practical knowledge. Many prepare you for professional certification or licensure. At the end of the program, you sit for an exam and earn a state-recognized certificate from a certifying agency or licensing board. If you are going for a professional certificate online, make sure that the program meets the certifying agency's or licensing board's requirements.

What's available in online learning professional certificate programs? Well, within the engineering profession, for example, there are certificates in computer-integrated manufacturing, systems engineering, and fire protection engineering. In business, there are online learning certificate programs in information technology and health services management. In education, online learning certificates are awarded in early reading instruction, children's literature, and English as a second language. In health care, certificates are awarded in medical assisting, home health nursing, and health-care administration. In law, distance learning certificates are offered in paralegal/legal assistant studies and legal issues for business professionals.

▶ THE FIRST ONLINE LAW DEGREE

For a long time, law degrees were not offered online. Students who wanted to enter the legal profession could get online certification for paralegal/legal studies and legal issues for business professionals but not law. However, indicative of the way online learning has opened up options for students, since 1998 Concord Law School has offered an online Juris Doctor (J.D.) degree and an Executive J.D.^{SM} It is the first institution to do so, and there are more than 1,700 students currently enrolled. Concord is registered with the California Committee of Bar Examiners, which permits its graduates to apply for admission to the California Bar. "This is a new phenomenon," says Barry Currier, Dean of Concord Law School. He points out that the online school is not trying to duplicate a residential environment, but the online program *does* deliver a law education to students who wouldn't normally be able to access it.

How we teach law online In traditional law schools, students have a case book with a set of cases and readings. They have class time. The curriculum is set up so that students read, go to class, and have discussions. We broke the class apart. We have the same books and the same reading assignments as regular law schools. We have videotaped lectures, accessible 24/7 on a Web site, by teachers who are good at lecturing and interacting with students. Students have readings, essays to write, and quizzes to take. All this is done asynchronously. There is synchronous class time with other students, which is audio streamed from the professor to the students and text-based back to the professor. Classes are conducted just as they would be in traditional law schools. We think the online classes are more engaging because, instead of just sitting in class, students get feedback and can watch and rewatch the lectures.

Barry Currier
Dean
Concord Law School

CONTINUING EDUCATION UNITS

Online learning is a great option for working adults whose professions require continuing education, even after they've earned their degree, certification, or license. Many states mandate continuing education for people in teaching, nursing, and accounting. Professionals in engineering, business, and computer science may opt to keep up with developments in their fields through online learning. If you take an online course for professional enhancement, you don't necessarily have to earn regular college credits for it. Instead, you may be able to earn Continuing Education Units (CEU). The CEU system is a nationally recognized program that provides a standardized measure for participation in continuing education programs. One CEU is defined as 10 contact hours of participation in an organized continuing education experience under responsible sponsorship, capable direction, and qualified instruction. Some institutions will permit you to take courses for continuing education credits rather than for regular credit or no credit. However, for proper recognition from employers and professional agencies, it is still important to take the courses from an accredited program.

CERTIFICATE PROGRAMS IN ACADEMIC SUBJECTS

Students who want to try on an academic subject for size, so to speak, can do so in an undergraduate or graduate certificate program in many academic subjects. You might take a few courses because you are heading down a different career path or because you were always interested in zoology and never got around to studying it. Many online learning providers, such as the University of Maryland University College, offer certificate programs in subjects like accounting, workplace Spanish, and bioinformatics.

Say you already have a bachelor's degree in computer engineering and go to work for a telecommunications company. After a few years, you realize that the financial sector really interests you. Instead of making an immediate career switch, you decide to take a few courses in business economics so that when you do decide to leave engineering for a financial services company, you'll have some knowledge about the industry. You might even decide later on to get a master's in economics. This, again, is one of the many reasons why it's important to make sure that the credits you earn in a certificate program for academic subjects will apply later if you do go into a degree program.

INDIVIDUAL COURSES

Students seeking to update their professional skills, acquire specialized knowledge, earn a few credits toward a degree, or simply take a class for pleasure can take individual courses online. Many institutions of higher education offer classes in various departments.

Summer Courses

Students in traditional colleges and universities are finding many opportunities to take summer courses online to help satisfy degree requirements. If their institution does not offer suitable online classes, they may be able to take online courses during the summer from any regionally accredited college or university and earn credit that can be transferred to their original institution.

. . . .

"We have students who aren't affiliated with Virginia Tech taking online summer courses and transferring them back to their own universities. Since 1999, we've put together an array of summer courses for undergraduate and graduate students in core areas. Our students who are here full time can pick up an extra course or, in some cases when they didn't do too well, take the course over. It helps reduce the time to graduation. Or, if they missed taking a prerequisite course that is only offered face-to-face once a year, they can take it online so that they're not put back a whole year."

Thomas W. Wilkinson
Director
Institute for Distance and Distributed Learning
Virginia Polytechnic Institute and State University

. . . .

Many colleges and universities require that you obtain a minimum number of credits from core courses and courses in your major at their institution in order to earn their degree. Check with your academic adviser and work out a degree plan before taking courses from other institutions.

Trying Online On for Size

If you are not yet enrolled in a degree program but think you might like to be in the future, taking a few online classes for credit is a good way to see whether or not an institution's online program suits your needs. If you find it does, you may be able to apply the credits toward your degree.

. . . .

"Before you decide to sign up for an online course, take an easy class online first. If it's in your major, you don't want to take higher level classes first. However, each online class is set up differently and has its nuances, like how you post assignments or check e-mails, so you'll have to relearn a few things in each new class you take."

Ryan Smith
Master's Student
Computer Information Systems and Web Design
University of Denver, University College

. . . .

NONCREDIT COURSES

Some people just want to learn and don't care about building credits toward a degree. A class here and a class there will pique their interest and off they go. Since each online learning program has its own policies about auditing classes, don't assume you can. Be sure to find out if the online learning provider you are considering allows you to audit classes without paying tuition. At Penn State World Campus, for instance, students must pay full tuition to audit a class, as they are required to submit all lessons and take all examinations (which are graded and returned). The notation on the transcript is AU and no college credit is earned.

JUST FOR FUN

Online learning isn't only for serious pursuits of education and training. Online learning has produced myriad fun classes and courses for children and adults. The subject matter is all over the place. Do you want to learn about your family's genealogy? How about hummingbirds, lighthouses, gardening, astronomy, or travel?

Businesses offer online classes. Verizon, for instance, has classes to teach students how to work with adult literacy learners. Fabric and craft stores teach quilt making online. You can learn how to take better digital photos: You receive a lesson, via e-mail, and a photo assignment and have two weeks to take the picture. The instructor looks at your photo and gives his or her comments and suggestions.

· ·

"People don't want their brains to go stale. That is what is important to me as an older student. You can learn anything online, like underwater basket weaving. I have such a thirst for knowledge that I keep pursuing it."

Patti Jennings
Bachelor's Student
Library and Information Systems
University of Illinois at Springfield

· ·

▶Part III

HOW Does Online Learning Work?

Search

Chapter 6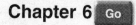

How You Learn Online

You might find it difficult to imagine what being in a "virtual class" is like. How can sitting in front of a computer monitor compare to the classroom experience? How can face-to-face interaction between students and teachers be equaled? Some say it can't. Others argue that online learning is not only as good as but is actually better than learning in traditional classrooms. However, for those who want an education but cannot physically attend a class, the argument is irrelevant.

HOW CLASSES ARE RUN

You will come across the terms *synchronous* and *asynchronous learning* in the context of online learning. In synchronous learning, classes and participation by students and teachers are scheduled at regular times. Asynchronous classes have no scheduled meeting time. Students log in whenever they choose to participate in online discussions, pick up and hand in assignments, and take tests. Online courses lend themselves to both synchronous and asynchronous learning.

Online class lengths vary greatly from five to ten to fourteen weeks. Independent learning classes take longer. At Rio Salado College, the "Survey of English Literature After 1800" class lasts fourteen weeks. Students taking "Effective Business Writing" at Penn State World Campus have up to eight months to complete the course at their own pace. At the University of Denver, University College, classes can run from five to ten weeks.

| Teacher Feedback | Student Story | Student Feedback |

I take a new class every five weeks with an eight-day break between classes. My oldest son is earning his second master's degree at a face-to-face college with some of the same classes that I'm taking. But his classes last nine weeks. I take only five weeks to learn the same information he's learning in nine. My classes are jam-packed with the same requirements and my mind is jam-packed too, but you get used to assignments due every other day or major assignments due every week.

Danny Cohen
Bachelor's Student
Information Technology
University of Phoenix Online

"Personally, I feel that online learning can be just as effective as traditional learning. It depends on the methods in which the instruction is delivered and the course structure."

Ronda Henderson
Ph.D. Student
Career and Technical Education
Institute for Distance & Distributed Learning, Virginia Tech

HOW YOU GET COURSE MATERIALS

Online students get materials for their classes in a variety of ways. Some teachers post the list of required textbooks online and students then purchase them online. In some cases, teachers put most of the text for the course online. "Our English 101 and 102 are going to be textbook-less," says Cynthia Maxson, who is on the English faculty at Rio Salado College. "All the information for the class will be online, including Web sites. This is very new. The students won't have to buy many books, just typically a handbook."

HOW ONLINE CLASS DEMONSTRATIONS AND FIELD TRIPS ARE CONDUCTED

The software available for online classes has developed to the point where demonstrations are not only possible but perhaps far more effective. This is particularly true for computer science students who can easily follow an instructor's movements on their monitors and then attempt the task themselves. "The notion of show me, teach me step-by-step, and then let me try in learning applications is a tremendous way to teach," says Ernest Eugster, Academic Director of Computer Information Systems at the University of Denver, University College.

For field trips, students "visit" various Web sites and are required to take copious notes for discussion of their observations at a later time. Or they can be sent to interview people or visit sites in their own communities.

HOW HANDS-ON LEARNING, PRACTICUMS, AND PROJECTS ARE FACILITATED

It would seem that, because students can't physically work together, group projects would be difficult to do online. This is not the case. Engineering and business students regularly collaborate on projects—sometimes even from different countries. It's common for medical students and pilots to learn via computer simulation in a low-risk environment. Online learning picks up the technology so that, as part of a course, you may have a three-dimensional simulation on your monitor that you can manipulate. Some online chemistry classes, for instance, allow students to conduct lab experiments online. Computer science courses are a natural for simulation and remote hands-on lab work. Eugster mentions several hosted environments that the University of Denver, University College, offers their computer science students. Using databases and operating systems that students download, students do exercises and then send in reports on the results.

Some courses, such as nursing and teacher education, require a hands-on practicum for which students may have to periodically come to classes on campus. Mary T. Champagne, RN, Ph.D., Dean Emeritus and Associate Professor, School of Nursing and School of Medicine at Duke University, notes that, with few exceptions, students in their programs must come to campus for concentrated periods to work with faculty members and other students for one to two days. "We find it important for students to make that interpersonal connection," she says.

Teacher training requires hands-on learning with students in a classroom. "You can't train people to do human interaction without human interaction," says Janet Johnson, Ph.D., Chair of Education at Rio Salado College. Education students are placed in local schools for their practicums and student teaching. Here they observe teachers, tutor students, prepare lessons plans, and teach in a supervised setting. Rio Salado College offers master-teacher seminars that students attend in person so that they can learn firsthand from experienced teachers what it is really like in the classroom environment.

Teacher Feedback | Student Story | Student Feedback

Online teamwork pays off

Distance education, in and of itself, can run counterproductive to teamwork and cooperation. Building online teamwork and cooperation requires design and deliberate strategies. But it does work. I do believe online teamwork is harder than doing it in person, even when we bring folks to campus so they can become acquainted before tackling their online teamwork. But I've had alums tell me they were put into various project-leader positions with their vendor companies because they already knew how to work in virtual teams and with customers at multiple sites and other coworkers at various geographical locations. This was an essential skill.

Linda Goodwin, RN, B.C., Ph.D.
Director, Nursing Informatics Program
Community and Family Medicine
School of Nursing
Duke University

▶ A LAB IN YOUR KITCHEN

If you sign up for the first semester of a first-year chemistry online course at the University of North Carolina at Wilmington, don't be surprised when Associate Professor Jimmy Reeves tells you to buy a $10 thermometer, get out your measuring cups, and clear off your kitchen table. Your kitchen is your lab. He's not kidding. He's found that students can conduct the same kinds of simple experiments in their kitchens as students can in a school lab, using ingredients like baking soda, vinegar, corn starch, and food coloring. While you won't get the same precision as you could in a lab, Reeves maintains that, for beginning chemistry students, getting the exact answer isn't as important as what is learned from conducting the experiment.

In the classes that follow this first-semester online course, students come into an actual lab with more sophisticated, precision equipment. Reeves has found that his online students make the transfer quite easily and actually have a greater understanding of the concepts than his face-to-face, in-the-classroom students.

HOW YOU CONDUCT RESEARCH AND GET INFORMATION

Research is a major part of learning. Knowing how to evaluate information—what is worth keeping and what is junk—is a valuable skill for all students whether online or on campus. Since online students might not have a college or university library nearby, online sources could be very important. However, some journals and scholarly works are not available online. Fortunately, many institutions that have online classes have interlibrary loan systems. So if students need a resource that is not available online, they can get it through the nearest library in the system. Some institutions will even send resources by courier to students' homes or offices.

▶ DON'T PLAY AROUND WITH PLAGIARISM

The Internet not only made it easy for students to access information, it also opened a Pandora's Box of plagiarism. Online schools take the issue very seriously. Teachers of online and face-to-face classes are quickly finding ingenious ways to counteract the numerous methods by which students pass off the work of others as their own. For instance, Turnitin.com is one service that many faculty members use to ensure that what a student has written is original or properly cited and not just lifted from a Web site. The service compares each student's work with more than a billion papers. At the University of Maryland University College, online students are required to take a tutorial that educates them about plagiarism. "Lots of people think if they copy materials from Web sites they don't have to attribute them," says Kim Kelley, M.L.S., Ph.D., Associate Provost and Executive Director of the Center for Intellectual Property, University of Maryland University College. She notes that this is a big issue. There are few Web sites where students can just copy materials without attribution.

HOW YOU ARE GRADED, QUIZZED, AND TESTED

When online students log in to class for the first time, they are likely to find a page detailing what is expected of them and how they'll be graded. For instance, in an online English composition class they will see exactly how many points will be given for organization, sentence structure, and mechanics, as well as how their participation in online class discussions and the quality of their responses are evaluated. Online teachers have many ways to keep track of the progress of their students and to ensure they aren't lost in the fray. Some online providers have online grade books that show students their grades and comments from the teacher. To give feedback on student essays, Cynthia Maxson at Rio Salado College uses different fonts in different colors. She might note something about the wording or use of verbs in the essay and write about the student's overall understanding of the assignment.

Those who remember taking a test or quiz in a class and then agonizing over their grade will love online classes. Online teachers can use test software that gives students instant feedback. In addition, some versions of testing software even point students to the pages in the textbook where they can brush up on information they missed on the quiz they just took.

Teacher Feedback | Student Story | Student Feedback

You really can't cheat

Having another student do the work instead of the student who is registered in an online class is almost a myth. Teachers get to know their students and interact with them. Often, assignments aren't graded, so students have no motivation to cheat, but teachers do get a sense of a student's writing style. Students have to write notes and participate in live, synchronous chats. Teachers sometimes see students or talk to them on the phone. If students have a proctored exam, they have to show evidence of who they are. If students write essays on tests that don't match up with other papers they've written, teachers will know. Students might be able to get away with it for a while but, ultimately, their work in courses will be measured.

Kim Kelley, M.L.S., Ph.D.
Associate Provost, Executive Director
Center for Intellectual Property
University of Maryland University College

"The first thing people ask is me is, 'Can you cheat?' Everything is open book so looking things up is not the issue. But if you have an hour for the test and three books, each with 300 pages, you can't cheat."

Patti Jennings
Bachelor's Student
Library and Information Systems
University of Illinois at Springfield

Open-book exams are common in online learning, but don't think they are easy just because you're sitting at home without a teacher staring at you. You will likely have a time limit in which to take the test and when it's over, it's over. Usually the tests are essays rather than multiple-choice or true/false. For the midterm and final exams, online students often must find a proctored test site, such as a public library or nearby university or college, or a proctor, such as a pastor, rabbi, teacher, or some other professional. The online provider contacts the test-site proctor and ensures that the person taking the exam is the enrolled student. In some cases, students must pay a small fee to take an exam.

▶ A PEEK INTO AN ONLINE PSYCHOLOGY CLASS

If you are wondering what an online class is like, take a look at what students in this psychology class (offered during the spring 2005 semester at the University of Illinois at Springfield) got from Professor Karen L. Kirkendall at the beginning of the class. The following syllabus gives you an idea of what she expected of her online students and how her online class was structured.

COURSE DESCRIPTION
This course is designed to provide an overview of adolescent development. A number of developmental areas will be covered (e.g., physical, cognitive, emotional, social). A special emphasis will be placed on contemporary issues concerning the development of today's adolescent.

REQUIRED TEXT
Santrock, J.W. *Adolescence.* (10th ed.) Boston, Mass.: McGraw-Hill Publishing, 2005.
A study guide is available in the bookstore. It is optional but highly recommended.

BLACKBOARD
Our online classroom "Blackboard" will be used to provide access to study questions, lecture outlines and handouts, lecture notes,

exercises, announcements, study tests, and your grades. You can access "Blackboard" through the Internet at http://bb.uis.edu/. You will need to use your UIS logon and password to gain entry. If you do not know what these are, call Technology Support at 206-7357. Once you have logged on, you will find the course materials organized in the following way:

- **Announcements** Announcements concerning changes, additions, deletions in course materials, exam and final grade distributions, reminders of exam and paper due dates
- **Class Schedule** Schedule of reading assignments, due dates, exam dates
- **Course Documents** Folders for each chapter in the assigned text that include study questions, lecture outlines and handouts, lecture notes, exercises, media, and study tests
- **Assignments** Folders for your guidelines for the adolescent interview and the consent form
- **Communication** Discussion Board (for class discussion/ questions about course material) and Group Pages (for posting assignments and receiving feedback on those assignments)
- **Group Pages** Direct link to your Group Page
- **Discussion Board** Direct link to the Discussion Board
- **Student Grade book** Access to your exam and written assignment grades
- **Staff Information** Names and numbers of staff in the psychology program whom you may need to contact while enrolled in my course

EXAMS

There will be three (80-point) exams on lecture (50%) and text (50%) material. Each exam will consist of objective (multiple-choice) questions. The exams will be released on Monday morning (during the designated exam week) at 8:00 am. The exams will be due the following Sunday at 5:00 pm. The exams will be open book, open notes; however, the items will be applied in nature, requiring that you generalize what you have learned to a case or real-life scenario.

STUDY QUESTIONS

Study questions will be available on "Blackboard" for each chapter. When each of these questions is answered thoroughly, the answers will represent the population of material that will be covered by the exam. You are NOT required to turn these in.

STUDY TESTS

Study tests will be available for each exam. The items on these tests will represent the kind of items you will have on the exam. You are NOT required to turn these in.

EXTENSIONS

Extensions on exams will be given only in the case of illness or emergency. The instructor should be contacted before the due date of the exam. If a student fails to do this, he/she will NOT be allowed to have an extension. Only one exam extension will be allowed over the course of the semester.

CHAPTER EXERCISES

On "Blackboard" you will find exercises for each of the content areas (chapters in text) that correspond to the material in the text, lecture, or media. You are required to complete and turn in each of these exercises by the Sunday before each exam is to be released (see class schedule). Each exercise will be worth a total of 5 points and will be graded on a Pass/Fail basis. Exercises may be turned in early (and multiple times) in order to receive feedback. Early turn-in due dates are specified in the course schedule. Please send me an e-mail when you post an exercise before the early due date. All exercises should be posted on your Group Page in the designated forum. All exercises should be posted in a message box (you may cut and paste your work from a WORD document). PLEASE do not post exercises as attachments. You will need to check your Group Page for feedback and grades on exercises. Exercises will not be accepted after the final turn-in date for the exercise group.

ADOLESCENT INTERVIEW

A 50-point interview with an adolescent is required. Each student will structure his/her own interview, basing questions on a contemporary issue or topic. Guidelines for developing interview questions, performing the interview, and writing up your report are available under the "Assignments" forum. All interview questions (10–15 questions) must be approved by the instructor before the interview takes place. The last day to have interview questions approved is March 6 at 5:00 pm. Obtaining consent to interview an adolescent is a requirement of the interview. Consent forms should be faxed or mailed to me no later than April 8 at 5:00 pm. A five- to seven-page summary of the interview will be due on April 10 by 5:00 pm and 5 points will be deducted for each day it is late. If the summary exceeds the limit of seven pages, the remaining pages will not be reflected in the paper grade. This assignment should be typed, double spaced, and prepared according to APA format. Interview reports should be posted on your Group Page in the designated forum as an attachment.

CLASS PARTICIPATION

Twenty-five points will be given for active participation in class discussion and other course venues (course documents, Group Pages, Discussion Board). Class discussion will be held on the Discussion Board. There is required reading and an exercise for each week of class (see schedule). Participation scores will reflect how well a student is judged to have met this requirement.

TURNING IN WRITTEN ASSIGNMENTS

All of your written assignments (exercises, interview questions, interview report) will be handed in to me by being posted on "Blackboard." Please do not turn in any assignment (except consent form) via e-mail, fax, or regular mail. Assignments must be posted on "Blackboard" by the designated deadline. You will post your assignments on a Group Page that I have established in the Communication menu option (there is a menu option that is a direct link to the Group Pages). Look for a Group Page that is labeled "Turn in your last name." There is a "turn in" Group Page for each student in the class, which allows access by only the student and me. Early turn-ins are allowed for all assignments. However, you must notify me by e-mail when you have posted an assignment on your Group Page prior to a deadline.

DISCUSSION BOARD AND E-MAIL

The Discussion Board for our class has been established to allow for questions and discussion concerning assignments and course content. I have already established a number of "forums" that allow for questions and discussion of the course requirements and syllabus, the adolescent interview, and content from the text chapters and lecture materials. Initially, I will post a discussion "thread" for each of the chapters. Students may respond to this "thread" or start their own discussion "thread." Please use the Discussion Board to ask all questions except for those that are of a personal nature. By using the Discussion Board, others can benefit from the answer to your question. The answer may come from me or from another student. Obviously, this is not the place for discussions of a personal nature (e.g., difficulties getting assignments in on time, illness, grade issues, problems with your computer). Please use e-mail (or your "turn in" Group Page) for these private discussions. You should try to post something to the Discussion Board at least two to three times a week. Here are some suggestions on the content and quality of these postings:

- Your postings should contribute to the ongoing discussion. Postings such as "I agree" or "That's a great comment" do not necessarily contribute to the discussion.
- Your postings should be courteous and respectful toward your peers and me.
- Postings should be relevant to the discussion. If you want to change the topic, start a new discussion "thread."
- Keep postings in the appropriate forums. For instance, do not ask technology questions in the middle of a content discussion.
- Keep postings to a reasonable length. Please try to keep them under three short paragraphs.
- Please try to attend to spelling and grammar in your postings. We all tend to make goofy mistakes when typing; however, these mistakes should not interfere with the ability to understand your point.
- Please keep postings timely. There is a reading schedule specified in the course schedule and everyone should try to keep to that schedule. Some discussion may go longer than a week—and that is okay. However, if you failed to contribute to the discussion that was three weeks prior, you should not try to backtrack.

GRADING SYSTEM

Exam grades will be determined by the following cutoffs: 90%—A, 80%—B, 70%—C, 60%—D. The highest score for each exam will set the cutoffs. Final grades will be determined similarly using the above cutoffs; the highest total will set the cutoffs for the final grades. You may access all of your grades on the online "grade book." I will post exam distributions as an announcement after everyone has completed the exam. Incompletes will only be given if you have had an emergency during the last part of the semester and cannot complete one of the assignments or exams. Incompletes will not be given so that you may repeat the course.

TECHNOLOGY PROBLEMS

Your main support system for technology problems is Technology Support at 206-7357. You will need access to Word™, PowerPoint™, and Realplayer™ to access course materials. Technology Support will be offering "Blackboard" training during the first week of class (I will post an announcement when I know these dates). "Blackboard" is a Microsoft product and you will need to use corresponding Microsoft products (Word, PowerPoint) or convert your documents.

STUDENTS WITH DISABILITIES

Reasonable accommodations are available for students who have a documented disability. Please notify the Office of Disability Services during the first week of class of any accommodations needed for the course. Late notification may cause the requested accommodations to be unavailable.

CLASS SCHEDULE

Week of	Reading and Exercise Assignments	
January 10	Introduction	Chapter 1
17	Science and Adolescent Development	Chapter 2
24	Biological Foundations	Chapter 3
31	Cognitive Development	Chapter 4
	DUE: Early Turn In for Exercise Group #1 (Chapters 1–5) February 6 at 5:00 pm	
February 7	Self and Identity	Chapter 5
	DUE: Exercise Group #1 (Chapters 1–5) February 13 at 5:00 pm	
14	Exam #1 (Chapters 1–5)	
	DUE: February 20 at 5:00 pm	
21	Gender	Chapter 6
28	Sexuality	Chapter 7
	DUE: Interview Questions by March 6 at 5:00 pm	
March 7	Moral Development	Chapter 8
	DUE: Early Turn In for Exercise Group #2 (Chapters 6–10) March 13 at 5:00 pm	
14	Holiday	
21	Families	Chapter 9
	Peers	Chapter 10
	DUE: Exercise Group #2 (Chapters 6–10) March 27 at 5:00 pm	
28	Exam #2 (Chapters 6–10)	
	DUE: April 3 at 5:00 pm	
April 4	Schools	Chapter 11
	DUE: Consent forms by April 8 at 5:00 pm	
	DUE: Adolescent Interview by April 10 at 5:00 pm	
11	Achievement	Chapter 12
18	Culture	Chapter 13
	DUE: Early Turn In for Exercise Group #3 (Chapters 11–14) April 24 at 5:00 pm	
25	Adolescent Problems	Chapter 14
	DUE: Exercise Group #3 (Chapters 11–14) May 1 by 5:00 pm	
May 2	Exam #3 (Chapters 11–14)	
	DUE: May 8 by 5:00 pm	

How Teachers Teach Online

Learning online isn't as different from learning in a traditional classroom as you may think. Just about every facet of a traditional classroom can be found in the virtual setting, except the physical presence of students and teachers. People already are comfortable with many of the elements and tools used in online learning. Anyone who communicates via e-mail knows how to exchange thoughts in writing, rather than verbally. Virtual meetings, similar to what takes place in an online class, are common in business settings with people in distant offices participating through a speaker phone or video cameras.

Online students will find that classes are taught in, essentially, three different ways: instructor-led, instructor-facilitated, and independent/self-paced learning. Students in classes that are instructor led have the least control over what is learned and when homework is turned in. The independent/self-paced classes are just what they sound like—students have the most control. There are pros and cons of each, so it's to your advantage to be familiar with each online teaching method when you are researching online learning programs and individual classes.

INSTRUCTOR-LED CLASSES

Most people are accustomed to instructor-led classes. Students meet in a specified place for a given amount of time. Online learning classes that are instructor led are no different. The teacher determines how the class is paced and sets a weekly schedule to which students must adhere. Students listen to lectures and take notes. In traditional class settings, a student's notes are normally the only record of the lecture. In online lectures, and even in some traditional classes, teachers post their lecture notes and PowerPoint presentations online so students can refer back to them. Everyone learns at the same time and at the same pace. Teaching in the online instructor-led classroom is supplemented by outside research and reading or by guest lecturers.

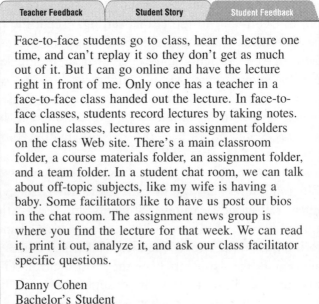

| Teacher Feedback | Student Story | Student Feedback |

Face-to-face students go to class, hear the lecture one time, and can't replay it so they don't get as much out of it. But I can go online and have the lecture right in front of me. Only once has a teacher in a face-to-face class handed out the lecture. In face-to-face classes, students record lectures by taking notes. In online classes, lectures are in assignment folders on the class Web site. There's a main classroom folder, a course materials folder, an assignment folder, and a team folder. In a student chat room, we can talk about off-topic subjects, like my wife is having a baby. Some facilitators like to have us post our bios in the chat room. The assignment news group is where you find the lecture for that week. We can read it, print it out, analyze it, and ask our class facilitator specific questions.

Danny Cohen
Bachelor's Student
Information Technology
University of Phoenix Online

INSTRUCTOR-FACILITATED CLASSES

In instructor-facilitated classes, the instructor is more of a guide, rather than a "chalk and talk" teacher—there to direct students to sources, help with problems, and answer questions. Students are not "taught" by an instructor but rather are learning on their own from textbooks, text the teacher posts, and videos or resources outside the classroom. Students do the required work according to their own schedules and turn it in when it is called for.

. . . .

"Some online education is described as 'instructorless education' in which the instructor is more of a resource and doesn't have a major role. We have not found that to be successful. It's like an electronic correspondence course. Retention rates are not very good. On the other extreme is the instructor-led model where the faculty member drives the learning and there is a tremendous amount of interaction."

Brian Mueller
CEO
University of Phoenix Online

. . . .

SELF-PACED OR INDEPENDENT LEARNING

This type of distance learning is similar to instructor-facilitated classes but students have even less contact with the teacher. Correspondence courses fall into this model. Students are given materials, directed to resources, and learn independently. Many independent learning courses have no set starting or ending date, such as a semester or quarter. Students begin the course at any time and progress through the material at their own pace. For instance, some students might choose to get through a ten-week course in six weeks by doing the reading, finishing the assignments, and taking the tests well before the class officially ends. The length of time students have to finish the materials could be weeks or months, depending on the subject matter and instructors. Some correspondence courses require students to finish chunks of materials before taking the next step.

Teacher Feedback | Student Story | Student Feedback

Mixed opinions about online learning

Edwin R. Watkins is taking both face-to-face and online classes while pursuing a dual master's in telecommunications and computer information systems. He is a product specialist in data at QWEST Communications in Denver. When QWEST offered to pay for his master's degree in any course that was industry related, Watkins signed up at the University of Denver. Some of the classes were offered only online, but since he was in the information technology and computer field anyway, he liked working on the computer and interfacing with the Internet. However, he isn't totally pleased with some of the aspects of his online classes, especially the group dynamics. He misses the verbal, open atmosphere of a face-to-face classroom and being able to watch the body language and facial expressions of a teacher. To him, there is no spontaneity online because the medium of e-mail is a chat back and forth with a gap of time between thoughts. He thinks computer classes with an instructor and whiteboard in front of the students, who are sitting at individual computers, offer the best of both worlds. When you make a mistake, the instructor can walk over and help you. But online learning does offer neophytes in computers some advantages, too, as Watkins feels it forces them to be more independent: they can't fall back on the group and they have to figure things out for themselves.

HOW CLASSES ARE STRUCTURED

As in face-to-face classes, online learning offers great flexibility in how classes are structured. For example, online students can be admitted in cohorts *(cohorts are students going through a series of classes together as a group, unlike the "regular" college class situation in which students take classes as individuals)* and move from one class to another in groups of ten to twenty until the entire course is completed. Online master's nursing and business classes are often arranged in cohorts. Or, as in a traditional class structure, students sign up for a course and when it's filled the class closes. Synchronous online classes tend to be smaller than the traditional undergraduate core classes where 200–300 students fill a lecture hall. This is because online teachers keep track of individual students via e-mail, which can become unmanageable with too many students.

Webinar is a term you will probably run across. It is short for *Web*-based sem*inars* in which students participate through their Web browsers while listening on the telephone to the teacher or visiting lecturer or even a panel discussion. Webinars can be highly interactive. Sometimes students participate by typing in their views or questions. Other times they can speak with the teacher and other students. Webcasts, on the other hand, do not allow for interaction and are set up only for students to view and hear.

▶ A SAMPLING OF ONLINE CLASSES

Using her experience as Course Development Team Leader at the University of Texas TeleCampus, Jennifer Freeman compiled this overview of how different online classes are set up. Of course, each online provider structures classes differently, but her list below gives you an idea of what you will generally find.

A math class usually is designed as a linear progression from easier topics to more difficult. Teachers may use java applets, animations, or drill-and-practice exercises. Students usually are assessed objectively with multiple-choice or true/false tests and homework problems.

An English composition class requires lots of reading, writing, and interaction from the students and often makes extensive use of a threaded discussion tool. Peer evaluation and "buddy writing" systems are common. Assessments are usually subjective (essays, papers, research, and discussions).

A language class requires lots of reading and writing from the students and usually includes audio/video, drill-and-practice, and homework assignments. Assessment plans often use both objective and subjective evaluations.

A history class may be very linear and structured or more open, depending on the instructor's teaching style and the target audience. It usually requires lots of reading, writing, and interaction from the students and often makes extensive use of a threaded discussion tool. Assessment plans use both objective and subjective evaluations.

A science class usually is designed as a linear progression from easier topics to more difficult. It may use java applets, animations, media, or drill-and-practice exercises. Students usually are assessed objectively (multiple-choice or true/false tests and homework problems).

An engineering class usually is designed as a linear progression from easier topics to more difficult. It often makes use of java applets, animations, and/or multimedia. Peer evaluation, group projects, and "study buddy" systems are common. Students are usually assessed objectively (multiple-choice or true/false tests and homework problems).

A class with many shared projects could be an M.B.A. program, for example. Although not required to, students often take courses as an informal cohort and get to know each other well. The courses usually require case studies or semester projects to facilitate critical thinking. These often are assigned as group or team projects.

A class that demands hands-on practical experience, such as nursing, is usually offered as a "hybrid" course—students use the online portion of the course for text-based activities and assessment but are required to participate in clinical activities to demonstrate their mastery of the material. These clinicals are usually proctored situations in a local hospital or lab.

Undergraduate courses are usually very structured, while graduate courses are less so in organization and content presentation, as students are expected to take responsibility for their own learning.

HOW CURRICULA ARE DEVELOPED

Students who have been in traditional college classes may find "comfort" in online programs that provide standardized courses, sometimes referred to as "signature" courses. Signature courses are typically developed by a team consisting of content and instructional design experts. Thus, while a number of faculty members teach and/or facilitate these online courses, students are assured of receiving standardized course content. For instance, at Rio Salado College, there is only one version of every course. So, students who are enrolled in the signature course for ENG 101 are assured of receiving the same course content, even though twenty different faculty members are teaching the course.

At the other end of the spectrum, professors in traditional colleges and universities have the academic freedom to develop a class and deliver the material as they see fit.

Online learning providers have one version of each class in order to take control of the content and the quality out of the hands of individual teachers. "How do you scale thirty-five versions of Psychology 101 and make sure it works?" questions Carol Scarafiotti, Executive Consultant, Online Learning, and Vice President Emeritus, Rio Salado College. She points out that they have classes starting every few weeks instead of the traditional semester or quarter, so they must ensure that every student has the same version of any course they sign up for. "All students enrolled in a particular course have the same course content and instructional design," notes Scarafiotti.

Some might argue that a standardized curriculum takes away the variables that enrich lectures given by a tenured professor who can choose when and what he or she wants to teach. However, with standardization, course developers can identify learning objectives and outcomes, ensuring that students get the education they are paying for, no matter who is teaching the course.

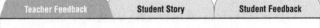

| Teacher Feedback | Student Story | Student Feedback |

Yes, you can teach art online

Let's say you're taking an art class. Classes are organized in 5½-week segments and are limited to 15 students so that teachers can maintain the volume of discussion threads. Interaction between students is key. In week one there are lecture materials to read but these are broken up with graphics since we're dealing with visual learners. Class facilitators add additional resources from the Internet to supplement the class. On a weekly basis, students are required to submit assignments and give substantive discussion. The FTP (file transfer protocol) technology allows students to scan their work and post it to the Web site for discussion. Students hold critiques on their work. In the introduction-to-drawing class, students have lectures and demonstrations on how to draw an object. They work independently and scan their work and submit it. It is reviewed by a facilitator and then posted so the other students can give their feedback.

Jenna Templeton
Director, Online Services
The Art Institute of Pittsburgh Online

"Technology has changed the stigma that artists draw and paint in dingy studios. The sophistication of software and the newer editions that are brought out have rapidly increased the quality of students' work produced on computers."

Edward A. Gill
Vice President, Academic Affairs
The Art Institute of Pittsburgh Online

How You Interact Online

Forget about keeping your head down and your mouth shut in an online class. Although the level of interaction in each class varies by the online provider, as well as by subject and teacher, face-to-face students have a much easier time of it: showing up for class, occupying a chair for 50 minutes, and leaving without saying a word. Many online students report that communication is much better for them than in traditional classrooms because teachers quickly note who speaks up, who takes over a conversation, and who keeps quiet and doesn't participate.

But that's not to say all online classes have high levels of interaction. Some classes are not designed to be highly interactive and, unfortunately, some teachers just aren't that responsive. Students do tell horror stories of teachers who take their sweet time responding to frantic e-mails and telephone calls or just post their PowerPoint lectures.

· ·

"If students need extra help, I'm willing to do that. I'm online every day. If there's a question, I'm there to answer it immediately so the student isn't floundering."

Cynthia Maxson
English Faculty
Rio Salado College

· ·

INTERACTIONS WITH OTHER STUDENTS

Online class discussions are either synchronous or asynchronous. If asynchronous, students do not have to be online at the same time. Students post their observations or answers to questions on message boards within a given period of time, which could span days or weeks. If synchronous, students do need to be logged in at the same time to share information and comments. It can be difficult to get online students together at one time: imagine scheduling a mutually convenient time for twenty-five students who are in Italy, Iowa, and Iceland!

Teacher Feedback	Student Story	Student Feedback

I'm taking a managing information systems course online, and we've had a diverse cross section of class meetings. We have chat rooms where you chat with a keyboard. We have had e-live chats in which everyone logs on with the instructor. It's kind of like a teleconference. I had to buy a mike. Once you start talking, a red icon comes on the monitor so you can't be interrupted. When you release a button, others can come in. We have the ability to raise our hands electronically.

We have all gotten an agenda so we come prepared with answers. There is no video of the participants or the teacher but we do hear each other's voices. The teacher puts up a PowerPoint on a whiteboard to facilitate the discussion and he'll pause and ask for comments while he's showing it. You would think it would be a messy free-for-all, but after we get the hang of it, everyone gets a chance to talk. The teacher keeps score so that if he sees someone is too passive, he'll get the student involved.

John Bohn
Master's Student
Business Administration
Nova Southeastern University

Mark Kretovics, Assistant Professor of Higher Education Administration at Kent State University, assigns reading that must be done by a certain day. The first week of class he posts notes to his students about what they've read and asks a series of questions. Students are expected to respond not only to his questions but also to what other students post in the same time period. After the first week of class, students must come up with their own questions about the materials they all have read.

Other teachers, like Duane B. Graddy, Professor of Economics and Finance at Middle Tennessee State University, may start a discussion with a lecture that students listen to as they watch slides or post an article online to get things going. For example, in a class on economic theory, the weekly topic might be to discuss the role of the economist in analyzing the costs of environmental pollution. Other classes use different methods. In a class on English novels, the weekly topic might be to discuss the role of the narrator or to analyze a specific passage. Students respond to the question and then to each other's comments. One of the advantages of threaded class discussions is that students are not bound by a 3-hour-class time limit.

Teacher Feedback	Student Story	Student Feedback

I like knowing what everyone is writing about. I can read abstracts from other students and question them and then add my thoughts to the discussion. In a class that lasts only 3 hours, you can't ask everyone what they're writing about or read what they're saying. But I can log on at 10 p.m. and get to know how others feel about a paper. We have a whole discussion posted so I can go back and reread it. You can't really miss a class either. On campus there's no way to go back and hear what was discussed, but in online learning what is discussed is posted, as are the questions that were asked.

Pami Ahluwalia
Master's Student
Computer Information Systems
University of Denver, University College

Karen L. Kirkendall, Associate Professor of Psychology at the University of Illinois at Springfield, places questions on a discussion and question board with links to lectures or class materials. Students are required to take part in the discussions, which she gets started and then tracks. If students want to start a side topic, they are welcome to label it. But, for the most part, they must relate their questions and answers to some application of the materials being discussed.

Teacher Feedback	Student Story	Student Feedback

The discussions are sometimes very interesting when they are done in the form of presentations by the professor. In these types of discussions, it is as if you are talking on the phone: you make a comment and you get immediate feedback. You are actually going through a presentation over the Internet and you can talk about the questions and give immediate feedback to other students. On the other hand, when you are working on an assignment or a project and you want to discuss an issue or concern, you can only rely on e-mail. That can be rather slow and not as effective.

Julio Aira Jr.
Master's Student
Business Administration
Nova Southeastern University

To allow multiple discussions about different aspects of a topic, teachers use software that breaks the threads into modules to prevent them from becoming unwieldy. Each thread is assigned a number and given its own area so that those who are following particular discussions can track their progression, instead of endlessly scrolling through text that has no logical separations.

Well-managed discussion boards keep to the topic. But then, not all teachers maintain successful discussions. Kretovics is very much involved in the dialogue that his students post and when he sees it going astray, he's quick to redirect it to the points he wants the students to learn. Susan G. Sharpe, Professor of English at Northern Virginia Community College, not only teaches online courses but she also took a noncredit course for homeowners who had wood lots and wanted to know how to manage them. The first time she logged on to the discussion board she found "100 students talking about whatever they wanted." Instead of discussing the tax implications of wood-lot ownership in Virginia, as they should have been, Sharpe found they were chatting about poison ivy and other unrelated subjects.

· ·

"For the most part, I received prompt feedback from the instructors via e-mail and telephone. But I have had instances where I felt 'out there alone in cyberspace' because the instructor rarely communicated with the students."

Ronda Henderson
Ph.D. Student
Career and Technical Education
Institute for Distance & Distributed Learning
Virginia Tech

· ·

Other elements can affect the success of online discussions. Class size matters a lot. Too many students, and you get overwhelmed with the number of responses you must read and react to. Too few students and the discussion soon peters out. Teachers must be careful in how they direct the discussion. If they go into too much detail about how they want the discussion to proceed, students are less likely to come up with creative insights of their own. Too few details and students flounder.

"I Liked Bob's Comments" Doesn't Impress Teachers

The quality and thoughtfulness of your participation in online discussions is a critical component to both your learning and your grades. Not only do effective online teachers look for the quantity of a student's replies, but they also scrutinize the content, even though it's a huge amount of work. Teachers often read 200 student responses a week for a class of twenty students.

Other teachers use discussions in place of research papers. Students are asked to read a series of articles and then give the class a one-page summary of the article and its implications. Not only do they get the feedback of other students, but they can see and learn from what others thought.

INTERACTION BETWEEN STUDENTS AND TEACHERS

Online teachers often set up a private group page that is accessible only to them and their students. Here is where students turn in assignments and exercises and where teachers provide individual feedback. Students can sometimes resubmit assignments, promoting one-on-one interaction between themselves and their teachers. Karen Kirkendall teaches face-to-face classes and, when comparing her interaction with her online students, reports that she interacts far more with her online students. Oddly enough, even though she has office hours for on-campus students, they seldom come by. Her classroom students turn in assignments and do the reading, but the only indicator she has that they're not keeping up is when exam time comes. On the other hand, she closely monitors online student participation by looking at statistics that tell her just how many times each student is on the discussion board.

. . . .

"Students expect online teachers to be online at least as much as they are. In a ten-week course, I sent or received more than 3,000 e-mails, which averages out to about 300 per week."

Nathan Kahl
Instructor, Euclid Program
Stevens Institute of Technology Web Campus

. . . .

INTERACTION WITH MENTORS AND TUTORS

Quality online providers realize that many students are wary of the whole online process, while others need special tutoring in subjects to help them get into the college study mode. Students beginning online courses at Penn State World Campus get an e-mail letter from an adviser who offers assistance. Once the students are ready to start classes, the adviser helps them navigate the online system. "We are their portal to the university. We are knowledgeable about the school's policies and programs," says Karen M. Lesch, Academic Advisor at Penn State World Campus.

She and the other advisers are liaisons, available from 8 a.m. to 9 p.m. Monday through Thursday to help online students with issues or problems, such as understanding why courses didn't transfer or helping select classes. They put students in contact with offices in the university if they need help with specific problems, such as students with disabilities or financial aid questions. Online students often need assistance getting around virtual libraries. Online providers with good student services have virtual librarians to help students get the resources they need.

Because so many students are adult learners who have been out of school for a long time, online learning providers often have brush-up courses in subjects like math, chemistry, or English.

Stevens Institute of Technology started providing courses for incoming freshmen who wanted to warm up in precalculus before starting their first semester. Some institutions provide 24/7 academic support by using outside companies where students can schedule regular tutoring sessions or submit papers for review and feedback.

▶Part IV

WHO Offers Online Learning?

Search

Online Learning— Everyone Is Doing It

As the number of people who want to learn online increases every year, so does the variety of institutions offering programs. An Internet search produces thousands of online learning programs— some legitimate, some not. Today's potential distance learners face a bewildering number of choices of institutions providing courses. Knowing which is which can make a difference when choosing the best online learning program for your needs.

Because of the significant differences among online providers, there are benefits and drawbacks to both traditional, nonprofit universities and colleges and for-profit, virtual online program providers. For instance, you might want to take only a few courses for professional development or just to learn something because you are interested in it and don't plan to transfer credits or seek a certificate. Or your whole future career could depend on getting a degree or certification.

TRADITIONAL AND NONPROFIT UNIVERSITIES AND COLLEGES WITH ONLINE LEARNING PROGRAMS

The most familiar group of online providers are the traditional colleges, universities, graduate schools, community colleges, technical schools, and vocational schools. In these institutions, distance education arose as individual administrators and faculty members took the initiative to use new technologies to deliver off-campus instruction to students. As the number of courses grew, many institutions developed whole degree programs as the next step.

. . . .

"Make sure this is what you want to do. Do the research. Ask questions. Talk to some people who have actually done this type of schoolwork. Just like the traditional schools, this is not cheap, so why pay back a loan for education without receiving a degree?"

Patricia Glenn
Associate Degree Student
Computer Information Systems
Kaplan University

. . . .

Public, nonprofit institutions have shown the most growth in online programs. The National Center for Education Statistics has some impressive numbers to substantiate this. They surveyed public and private two- and four-year colleges and universities in 1997–98 and 2000–01 and found the number of institutions offering distance education courses and the number of enrollments shot up in just three years. Public two-year colleges, for instance, went from 710,000 enrollments to nearly 1.5 million. In 1997–98, only 34 percent of postsecondary institutions offered distance education courses. By 2000–01, it had jumped to 56 percent. The Sloan Foundation and Babson College reported in 2003 that 81 percent of all the institutions of higher education in the United States provide students with "at least one single distance education course."

The Sloan Foundation also asked more than 1,100 colleges and universities if "online education is critical to long-term strategy." The results follow.

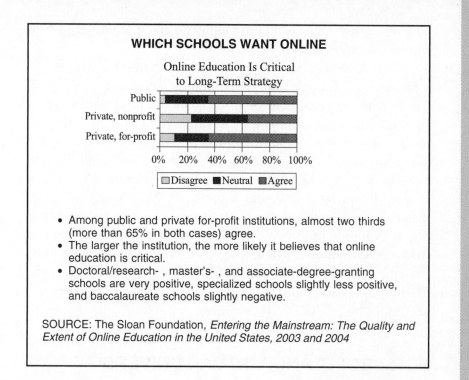

WHICH SCHOOLS WANT ONLINE

Online Education Is Critical to Long-Term Strategy

(Chart showing Public, Private nonprofit, Private for-profit with Disagree, Neutral, Agree categories on a 0% to 100% scale)

- Among public and private for-profit institutions, almost two thirds (more than 65% in both cases) agree.
- The larger the institution, the more likely it believes that online education is critical.
- Doctoral/research- , master's- , and associate-degree-granting schools are very positive, specialized schools slightly less positive, and baccalaureate schools slightly negative.

SOURCE: The Sloan Foundation, *Entering the Mainstream: The Quality and Extent of Online Education in the United States, 2003 and 2004*

The greatest advantage that most traditional colleges and universities bring to online learning is that they are established, well-known institutions with reputable faculty members and solid educational credentials. But many of the institutions that first offered online programs soon realized that developing viable online learning programs takes an enormous amount of resources in funds, faculty and staff members, and support services for professors and students. If they do not have high-quality online programs, it is likely to be in the areas of instructional and information technology. Recognizing this shortcoming, many colleges and universities have established policies and procedures to set up instructional technology standards and consistency and have increased their technical resources and training efforts to support faculty members and students.

Lori McNabb, Student and Faculty Services Manager at the University of Texas System TeleCampus, points out how tightly her department keeps control of the quality of its student services. By contract, faculty members are not allowed to have more than 20 percent of course materials on servers that are not managed by the University of Texas System TeleCampus Student and Faculty Services. It sounds like a minor point, but what happens if you're a student following a link that a professor has given you to get material for a class that is on another server and that server is down? Not only can't you get the information, but there's no one to call. "We want everything that is related to a course here to be something our Help Desk can help a student with at 3 a.m. in the morning. We can ensure that our servers are reliably maintained," says McNabb.

FOR-PROFIT AND VIRTUAL UNIVERSITY ONLINE LEARNING PROGRAMS

Another facet of the online spectrum is the for-profit, publicly traded institutions completely focused on online degree and course offerings. "There are thousands of for-profit institutions," says Jamie P. Merisotis, President of the Institute for Higher Education Policy, explaining that a for-profit institution has shareholders or is owned by an individual who runs it as a corporation. In between are the primarily online institutions that have students on residential campuses.

For-profit online providers are often called *virtual universities* because they are essentially schools, without campuses, delivering instruction and degree programs exclusively online or via other technical means. When the University of Phoenix Online began as an offshoot of the University of Phoenix in 1989, its goal was to provide practical education for the working adult to take and apply in the workplace. They now offer more than forty accredited degree programs in business, technology, education, health care, and more.

Walden University, founded in 1970, is an online provider that, from its inception, has been geared toward professionals and adults in the workplace who want to earn doctoral degrees. Similarly, the Cardean Learning Group (formerly UNext, Inc.) is a privately held corporation, originally formed to offer graduate business and management degrees. It has since formed an alliance with New York Institute of Technology, known as Ellis College of NYIT, and is an online provider serving working adults.

. . . .

"People have recognized, and will recognize, that traditional and nontraditional have to be rethought. Online education is becoming more traditional than what is thought of as traditional."

Brian Mueller
CEO
University of Phoenix Online

. . . .

WHAT DO THE DIFFERENCES AMONG NONPROFIT AND FOR-PROFIT MEAN TO YOU?

Name Recognition

It's hard to miss the pop-up and print ads enticing you to get a degree for this or that subject from this or that provider, but many of the provider names are not familiar. So, currently, traditional colleges and universities have the most name recognition.

Employers increasingly accept online degrees and certification, but the branding of a campus-based institution that has been around for a while is much greater than a for-profit, virtual school. However, as online learning becomes widespread and enrollments continue to rise, for-profit online providers should become recognized and accepted.

Faculty Members

Who will teach your course is perhaps one of the greatest differences among the different types of online providers. But even here, you can't make hard and fast delineations. In online courses offered by traditional colleges and universities, those who teach online are professors, primarily tenured, who also teach face-to-face classes. They are involved in research and publish within their own fields, bringing fresh knowledge about their subject areas to their students.

Many online for-profit institutions use adjunct faculty members who teach part-time. As professionals in the workplace, they bring practical, hands-on experience to the classroom.

. . . .

"The most important thing to students in an online course is a good instructor. Students will forgive weak course design. They will overlook some of the technical problems. But if you have a faculty member who engages the students and contacts them frequently, that faculty member will make the learning experience wonderful."

Carol Scarafiotti
Executive Consultant, Online Learning
Vice President Emeritus
Rio Salado College

. . . .

Curriculum

Another big difference among online providers is how the curriculum is developed. As previously mentioned, some institutions have centralized curricula. Teachers follow a curriculum within a set schedule. All students signing up for English composition or economics are taught the same information, in the same sequence, no matter when they enroll. In contrast, professors in traditional universities have academic freedom to decide what their students learn. They determine how the classes are taught and what to emphasize or leave out.

CORPORATE UNIVERSITIES

Corporations have long known about the benefits of online learning. Though training has always been an integral part of a profitable business, in the past it meant pulling employees away from their desks and often sending them to other locations for periods of time. E-learning changed all that. In fact, companies that customize and facilitate online corporate training for multiple businesses are numerous. "It's definitely growing," says Pat Galagan, Vice President of Content at the American Society for Training and Development. "With five years of data, we can see that classroom corporate training is descending and e-learning is ascending."

Sue Todd, President of Corporate University Xchange, says, "Each corporation typically has a number of programs they deliver." These include educating new employees on a company's mission and vision, professional development, and leadership development, which, Todd states, is the biggest category. According to Todd, corporations spend about $60-billion a year on training, a figure that is reduced with online learning. In addition to training employees for compliance and regulation purposes, corporations have seen the value of an educated workforce and many not only offer employees the option of pursuing online degrees but also pick up the cost.

K–12

Unless you have school-age children, you are probably unaware that online learning is revolutionizing education from kindergarten through high school, where it is used in classrooms to supplement and enhance learning. The U.S. Department of Education released figures from one of the first surveys to provide national data on distance learning in K–12, indicating that 36 percent of public school districts and 9 percent of public schools had students enrolled in distance education courses in 2002–03.

Barbara Stein, Senior Policy Analyst, External Partnerships and Advocacy at the National Education Association, notes that online learning in the lower grades is primarily part of the classroom curriculum. However, high school students can access classes that are not available at their schools and take advanced placement and other college-level classes without physically going to a college campus. "There's the recognition that, in remote areas, students don't have access to the variety of classes. Online education is a way to enhance the existing curriculum," says Stein. She notes that there is a smaller percentage of programs for homeschoolers and charter schools, but they, too, are increasing.

. . . .

"Many classes use interactive video. You are on one site and see the person at the other site, sort of like a teleconference. They see you. You see them. You push a button and they respond. Also there is some real-time Internet software where students can raise their hands and learn in real time. Increasingly, schools are using asynchronous online courses to enhance offerings. The flexibility of location and time actually provides important advantages for scheduling."

Barbara Stein
Senior Policy Analyst
External Partnerships and Advocacy
National Education Association

. . . .

About Consortia

With the Internet bridging the geographic gap, institutions in a state or region or those focused on a single subject area often band together to provide a wide variety of resources and courses that wouldn't be possible from only one provider in one location. Think of the myriad choices of specialized courses that were not available in your "home" college or university but were available in another school located hundreds of miles away.

When looking at various online providers, you will find that many of them are in partnerships called *consortia*. Consortia are associations of higher education institutions that have agreed to share online learning and resources, instead of duplicating efforts. They have become particularly powerful and influential in online learning. You will find this especially true for statewide consortia.

One of the important things to know about consortia is that they do not grant degrees. Students who apply to an institution that is part of a consortium can take courses from any of the other institutions in the consortium but receive their degree from the university or college to which they were initially admitted. A notable exception is the Western Governors University (WGU). Students apply to the WGU and, while they can take courses from any member institutions, their degrees are from the WGU, not any particular institution they attended.

WHY SHOULD YOU CARE ABOUT CONSORTIA?

If you don't check to see if the institution you plan to attend is part of a consortium, you could be missing out. For instance, consortia give you many more choices of courses and professors. With more than one institution offering online classes at different times, you can find not only the courses you need but also the times that suit your schedule. Instead of looking at a dozen catalogs to figure out what is where, consortia provide a central database of courses and schedules. If you are in a highly specialized field or profession and must find a faculty member with some particular knowledge, consortia offer a much wider selection. Because consortium members pool resources and expenses, students are likely to get a much higher level of student services, such as the ability to research a subject in five or six libraries via a digital library system.

Students aren't the only ones to benefit from consortia. Professors teaching online don't necessarily have the expertise to design their classes and teaching methods. As part of a consortium, faculty members have access to more extensive academic tools and services suited to teaching online. Institutions in consortia can offer cost-effective support to teachers, including instructional design and course development, faculty training, technical support, and policy development. As online departments grow, institutions find they must devote increasing resources to their teachers and students. "Consortia facilitate member organizations to do a better job by helping faculty members learn how to teach online courses, provide learner support, and apply best practices," notes Janet Poley, Ph.D., President of the American Distance Education Consortium.

FIGURING OUT CONSORTIA

With the diversity of online learning, consortia of online institutions are just as varied. Let's take a look at two main categories of consortia: statewide consortia and regional consortia. The following gives you just some examples of the different kinds of consortia you will find as you search for online learning program providers.

Statewide Consortia

These consortia include both public and private institutions of higher education. Students in the state can use a single Web site to select online courses offered by member institutions. Students enrolled in institutions in statewide consortia have access to online courses offered in other member institutions.

The SUNY Learning Network is an example of a statewide consortium. Students at SUNY Learning Network can choose from thousands of online courses, which are designed and taught by SUNY faculty members at participating campuses located around New York State. Online courses are available to degree-seeking students or to students who simply want to take courses for personal or professional development (nonmatriculating students).

A statewide consortium that does not provide degrees

The Kentucky Virtual University is the state's official virtual campus. It's a single access point for students all over Kentucky to more than twenty-five institutions, ranging from universities to technical colleges. Each member institution charges its own tuition rates for in-state and out-of-state students. Students can access academic programs from accredited postsecondary institutions in Kentucky and only have to fill out a common form to apply online to any one of its member institutions.

A statewide consortium of one university system

The University of Texas System Telecampus is a consortium of fifteen institutions within the University of Texas system. It facilitates delivery of more than twenty fully online programs; most of them are shared by all participating campuses. Students receive their diplomas from the university to which they applied.

Other states that operate consortia of their public colleges and universities include Colorado, Connecticut, Illinois, Kentucky, New Jersey, New York, Ohio, Texas, and Utah. All have arrangements in place whereby students can take some transferable courses online from more than one institution and apply them toward a degree at their home institution.

A statewide consortium supporting five different campuses
The University of Massachusetts UMassOnline links Amherst, Boston, Dartmouth, Lowell, and Worcester. UMassOnline allows students to connect directly to each campus to access course descriptions and get information about admissions, credit transfers, financial aid, prerequisites, registration, tuition, and academic advising.

A statewide consortium coordinating the state's community colleges and universities
The Florida Community College Distance Learning Consortium represents Florida's twenty-eight community colleges and eleven universities and private institutions accredited by the Southern Association of Colleges and Schools. It coordinates the development, delivery, marketing, and acquisition of online learning.

Regional Consortia

Institutions in regional consortia are located in more than one state and can incorporate public or private institutions or a mix of both. Regions can extend across national borders.

A regional consortium across sixteen states
The Southern Regional Education Board's (SREB) Electronic Campus calls itself an "electronic marketplace" of public and independent colleges in the south. States included in the SREB are Alabama, Arkansas, Delaware, Florida, Georgia, Kentucky, Louisiana, Maryland, Mississippi, North Carolina, Oklahoma, South Carolina, Tennessee, Texas, Virginia, and West Virginia. The SREB gives students access to select campuses and/or e-learning to match their needs. It is an online resource for students who want to attend traditional face-to-face classes.

A regional consortium of nine universities

The National Universities Degree Consortium (NUDC) connects nine universities in states as far apart as Missouri and Washington that offer associate to doctoral degrees via seventy distance programs. NUDC is a gateway for students and guarantees a standard of quality in the courses it lists by reviewing them to ensure they are well set up and supported by adequate services. It leaves the choice of curriculum content up to the individual member institutions.

A regional consortium supported by governors of 19 states

The Western Governors University is a nonprofit university offering online education and is the only accredited university offering competency-based online degrees from bachelor's to master's and licensure programs in teaching, business, and information technology. Unlike other virtual universities that serve as a hub or a consortium, WGU enrolls its own students and grants its own degrees by assessing students' knowledge through competency-based examinations. WGU does not teach its own courses, but it provides its students with access to courses from member institutions.

▶Part V

WHY Should I Consider Online Learning?

Search

The Pros and Cons of Online Learning

Thomas W. Wilkinson, Director of the Institute for Distance and Distributed Learning at Virginia Polytechnic Institute and State University, sometimes gets comments from parents who wonder why they have to pay full tuition for online courses. In their minds, online learning should be cheaper because they equate online with correspondence courses; after all, their children are not sitting in a classroom. Many think online means lower quality because they've seen diploma mill advertisements promising a degree that is "only a click away." Prestige and quality mean ivy-covered walls, not a desktop in the den. There is no doubt that a lot of people are still wary about online education.

As online learning becomes more popular and commonplace, the pros will eventually outweigh the cons. Research indicates that online learning is, in many ways, better than face-to-face. "The University of Central Florida surveys its online students every other semester. Using a C or better grade as a benchmark for success, we find face-to-face and online students are almost identical," says Peg Miller, Ph.D., Coordinator of Academic Support for Distributed Learning at the University of Central Florida.

ONLINE DISCUSSIONS VS. FACE-TO-FACE DISCUSSIONS

One of the more significant discussions about online learning swirls around the quality of interaction between students, students and teachers, and students and information. Some say that meaningful discussions can only effectively happen face-to-face. But Lori McNabb, Student and Faculty Services Manager at the University of Texas System TeleCampus, contends that if you don't want to get into discussions with classmates, online learning isn't for you. "Typically, in an on-campus class, a group sits in back of the room, takes notes, and never talks. In online classes, you must interact," she says. Students cannot avoid being dragged into conversations because online teachers track who is interacting, how many times they interact, and what they discuss.

. . . .

"I like to answer e-mail at least once a day so students get more feedback than in a class that meets two or three times a week. Students need not "store up" their questions. Both students and teachers can take time to consider what they are discussing; foreign-based students are especially happy to be able to work through language problems in a way that's impossible in a face-to-face class."

Keith W. Miller
Professor, Computer Science
University of Illinois at Springfield

. . . .

Advocates of online learning point out that discussions are not limited to 50 minutes. Shy students who wouldn't dream of raising their hands in class and are not good at thinking on their feet appreciate the time that e-mail discussion gives them. Faculty often comment that the depth of online discussions exceeds what they can achieve in the face-to-face classroom. Some faculty feel they know their online students as well, or better, because of that, says Jennifer Rees, Manager of Communication Services at the University of Texas System Telecampus.

Teacher Feedback	Student Story	Student Feedback

I've had online classes where the interaction has gone well. The students were involved in an interactive community. But I had a class with only a few students and it didn't work out as well. A lot of education comes from other people's experiences, so it can go both ways in an online class. It's really up to the professor to determine the success of the class.

Ryan Smith
Master's Student
Computer Information Systems and Web Design
University of Denver, University College

Many online teachers base part of the grade on student participation. Some require participation three to five times a week and not all on the same day. Teachers who know how to effectively manage online discussions can prevent aggressive and talkative students from dominating a conversation and easily steer a conversation toward their class goal.

. . . .

"When I was in a [face-to-face] class of 300 people, no one wanted to raise their hands and ask questions. But in an online environment, you don't mind sending e-mails. It's no big deal. People are not afraid to ask questions in e-mails."

Larry Keisler
Bachelor's Student
Organizational Leadership
Penn State World Campus

. . . .

A possible downside to online learning is the inability to detect body language, which is important, especially around exam time. Patti Jennings is an online student of Library and Information Systems at the University of Illinois at Springfield. In face-to-face classes, she picks up clues about what is important to the professor from what he stresses or gets excited about. When preparing for an online exam, she doesn't have those visual and auditory hints. Classes that are taught using real-time video and audio components negate that argument; however, not all courses have that type of software.

· ·

"It's tough not to hear a professor's point of view. I wouldn't want to see someone earn every degree online. Face-to-face communication can benefit people a lot. Some portion of undergraduate and graduate education should be in class. My master's is all online. I haven't had to set foot on a campus, but I did it [online] because I had to."

Terri Burris
Master's Student
Education
Virginia Polytechnic Institute

· ·

SOCIALIZING ONLINE VS. FACE-TO-FACE

"Increasingly, the questions about online learning are not about technology or learning, but more about the social environment," notes Gerald Heeger, President of the University of Maryland University College. Many argue that technology isolates people and online learning only adds to the problem. Undergraduate college students in particular don't go to college simply to acquire information leading to a career. During those four years on campus, they learn social skills and how to be adults and integrate into society. So, while younger students gain more from a face-to-face environment, between work and family, adult learners probably have more socialization than they can handle.

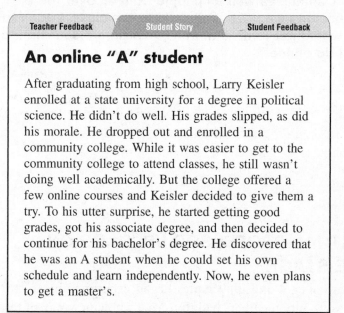

Teacher Feedback | Student Story | Student Feedback

An online "A" student

After graduating from high school, Larry Keisler enrolled at a state university for a degree in political science. He didn't do well. His grades slipped, as did his morale. He dropped out and enrolled in a community college. While it was easier to get to the community college to attend classes, he still wasn't doing well academically. But the college offered a few online courses and Keisler decided to give them a try. To his utter surprise, he started getting good grades, got his associate degree, and then decided to continue for his bachelor's degree. He discovered that he was an A student when he could set his own schedule and learn independently. Now, he even plans to get a master's.

One advantage to online learning that students cite is the diversity of their classmates. Since students can participate from just about any geographic location, classes often include people from other countries. Not only do students benefit from the experience of working on group projects with students outside the United States, but they also have the opportunity to get to know them personally.

. . . .

"In my class there's someone from Japan and someone from Canada, as well as people from all over the U.S. The discussions we have really add to the class. I don't think you would get to do that in a classroom discussion, but I feel I do online."

Pami Ahluwalia
Master's Student
Computer Information Systems
University of Denver, University College

. . . .

VIRTUAL PROFESSOR VS. SAGE ON THE STAGE

When colleges and universities began experimenting with online classes, faculty members had to learn a whole new way of teaching. They soon found that simply putting PowerPoint notes online or tweaking lectures they had used for years didn't work. Professors reported that going through the rigors of teaching students via the Internet forced them to reexamine how they teach. They had to step back from their familiar patterns and methodology. "We're making them recreate whole courses from the core. It's an entirely different mindset," reports Lori McNabb from the University of Texas System TeleCampus.

. . . .

"For my own personal situation, I prefer the classroom scenario. I am taking programming classes, which is a complex subject, and you need a lot of interaction with your instructors. I find face-to-face much more helpful. For the true distance learner who can't get to a classroom, online is an advantage, but, for someone who has the opportunity to be in a classroom, I think it's better. In the face-to-face graduate classes I've had, where there have been as few as four students, it's easy to say, 'Excuse me, I'm lost.'"

James O'Neill
Master's Student
Computer Science
University of Denver, University College

. . . .

Now that online learning providers have more experience in what works and what doesn't, faculty members use a wide variety of teaching strategies and platforms. Professors teaching online courses at Duke University's School of Nursing and School of Medicine, for instance, have the use of a recording studio. Other online providers, such as the University of Texas System TeleCampus, have a team of graphic designers, instructional designers, programmers, and animators who support the course material with their technical and creative talent. The professors do the teaching, but a backup team helps with everything—down to the fine details of checking links on Web pages to make sure they work. Each time the course is offered, the content and delivery are scrutinized and improvements are made before it is released.

In online courses, someone can monitor what's going on because classes are designed and built by experts in instructional technology. In addition, there is a written record of what has been posted. In face-to-face classes, the lecture hall door is closed and no one knows if the professor is reading twenty-year-old notes.

ONLINE LEARNING OUTCOMES VS. FACE-TO-FACE

Mark Kretovics, Ph.D., Assistant Professor in the Higher Education Administration Department at Kent State University, conducted a study comparing online and campus learners in an M.B.A. program at Colorado State University, where he was then Assistant Dean. The purpose was to test learning outcomes. The online class was 100 percent asynchronous, meaning that students could participate in class discussions at their convenience. The survey found that online students learned as well as, or better than, the face-to-face students. Kretovics admits he didn't expect the online learners to grasp the theories as well as the on-campus students, but they did. He concluded that the online environment fosters independent learning. Because students aren't guided by professors or pick up their biases, they depend on their own observations and conclusions in applying theories.

"There are lots of reasons for taking online courses. For example, the costs of getting to a campus might be too high. However, for many students, it's really a pleasure to be in a classroom. Most students would like a campus-based course because of the interaction, especially if it's a small class. The lecture classes I teach are often large. In such situations, there's not much interaction and not much contrast between online and face-to-face classes. But in a small class, students have lots of interaction, not just chalk and talk. They can often get a much fuller explanation of something when they can interact with a person."

John Dutton
Associate Professor, Business Management
College of Management
North Carolina State University

One would assume that students learning languages face-to-face would do much better than their online counterparts. When Vernon Smith first began teaching language online he, too, had his doubts, until he saw nationally normed test-score results for online students, which were the same as or better than campus-based students. Smith is currently Faculty Chair for Foreign Languages at Rio Salado College. At Rio Salado, language students are tested on reading, writing, speaking, and listening skills, as well as knowledge of the culture. Students have videos that demonstrate the language in context, including nonverbal aspects such as gestures, which are an important part of learning a language. They can listen to and view lessons multiple times so that the language is slowly absorbed by repetition and practice. The only disadvantage

Smith saw was the socialization aspect of language, which he, as an instructor, could overcome with online voice assessments and discussions.

▶ MIGHT AS WELL DISPEL SOME MYTHS ABOUT ONLINE LEARNING

Online learning is often one of those "ah-ha" experiences. You think you know about it, but once you get into it you find it is quite different from what you expected. Online learning is still being developed and refined, so some of these myths could be realities if program providers are not offering their students a quality education.

Learning online is easier than learning face-to-face. Nothing gets students into more trouble than thinking they can coast through an online course, pick up a decent grade, and move on to the next class. Once you take your first online class, you will know this is one of the top misconceptions about online education. First-time students often assume that because they don't sit in class for 3 hours a week they can scratch that time from their to-do list. They can't. Online students must study the 3 hours a week they would have been in class plus the 2 to 3 hours face-to-face students normally study outside of class. That's 5 to 6 hours a week per class.

The quality of online classes is lower than face-to-face classes. Maybe this was true when online learning programs first started. But it's not true anymore, unless you're looking at a diploma mill. (Chapter 14 discusses diploma mills in depth.) Nowadays, online programs from accredited institutions are rigorously designed. Quality online learning programs have entire departments dedicated to designing courses and training teachers. They constantly check course content and track teachers far more easily because everything—notes, lectures, demonstrations, student feedback, testing—is online.

I'll be out there in cyberspace on my own with no help. Experienced online programs include interaction and accountability with the teacher and other students in the course. Tech support is a vital part of good programs. Many programs offer help—either through the telephone or CDs—in familiarizing students with the software needed for their courses. Quality programs have advisers and mentors to assist you through the admission process and tutors to advise you in writing papers.

Online learning is for people in the wilds of Montana. Yes it is, and it's for working adults in metropolitan centers who don't feel like dealing with traffic and parking or students who want to take a course that is scheduled at a suitable time for them. Increasingly, students who live on campus sign up for online courses because they find them so convenient.

Online learning is just a bunch of e-mails back and forth. The software available to online learning providers has made the online educational experience amazingly similar to face-to-face. Students can see, hear, and respond to instructors as though they were in a classroom. Not every provider uses the very latest software but many do, and the online learning experience gets better with each new technological breakthrough.

I need to be a computer geek. Online course providers are well aware that unless online students can use the programs and easily move around in a virtual environment, they will become frustrated and drop out. Some providers have computer tutors who walk new students through the technology. Others have 24/7 help desks, so if you run into a technical glitch at 11 p.m. someone can help you fix it. Look at it this way: If you can order flowers or movie tickets over the Internet, you've got enough "geek" to be successful. But, if you are hesitant about computers, check out the program's help desk setup before signing on.

Online courses are cheaper. Sorry to say this is definitely a myth. Online courses cost the same as traditional college courses, if you attend a recognized institution. Read Chapter 16 for more information about paying for online courses.

Chapter 12 `Go`

So—Is Online Learning Right for You?

Online learning is not for everyone, even those who think it's great. Some people just learn better in a face-to-face environment. Online learning tends to suit adult learners, as they have the self-discipline and motivation that comes from maturity. There are reasons why the percentage of students who drop out, or stop out (drop out for a few semesters, or even years, and then drop back in), is high. People hear how convenient online learning is and don't realize the commitment it takes to be successful. They start a class, get behind a little, then more and more, and soon they're failing. Answering the following questions can help you determine if you and online learning are a good fit.

❶ Do you understand the demands of online learning?

Since online learning attracts adult learners, many of them have been out of school for some time and aren't used to being students again. Assuming online is easy, many students who are unfamiliar with online learning sign up for more courses than they can handle. They don't realize that along with convenience comes homework; mandatory participation in discussions; collaborating on projects, essays, and papers; and weekly quizzes.

· ·

"Realize that online learning is not 'a piece of cake.' If anything, it is more difficult and time-consuming than a traditional class. Understanding this concept from the beginning will make things smoother for you."

Ronda Henderson
Ph.D. Student
Career and Technical Education
Virginia Polytechnic Institute

· ·

❷ Can you turn off the TV and pick up a textbook that you're not interested in reading?

Time management is an essential skill often mentioned by seasoned online learners. Students who were at the top of their classes in high school, and never had to do much to stay there, often find themselves floundering in online classes because they can't manage their time.

For the most part, online students set their own schedules, in between picking up assignments from a Web site and turning them in by a designated time. "Online students have to realize they can't do the work only when they feel like getting around to it," says Claudine SchWeber, Ph.D., Chair of the Doctoral Program at University of Maryland University College. She teaches undergraduate and graduate classes online. Her classes are structured so that students have weekly reading assignments, activities, projects, quizzes, and mandatory discussions. They have to maintain the pace she sets in order to complete the course in a timely manner.

. . . .

"I was able to balance my school schedule around everything else in my life. I am a single parent with two children. I work in retail and take care of my elderly mother. In addition, I must always find time for me. I just do not think that I could have maintained the momentum in a traditional classroom environment. You can succeed in an online environment if you can plan and maintain your time."

Reneé Green
D. M. Student
Management Organizational Leadership
University of Phoenix Online

. . . .

③ **Are you a good procrastinator?**

If you need constant reminders to do a task, you're in trouble. Karen Kirkendall, Associate Professor of Psychology at the University of Illinois at Springfield, can spot procrastinators in her online classes. They're usually the students who could slide by in face-to-face classes and have never failed before. Most of her classes are very structured with well-defined times when work is due. In between, though, students can work at their own pace. Procrastinators think they can scramble and get assignments done, but they end up falling into a downward spiral. "Students end up having bad grades before they realize it's happening," says Kirkendall, pointing out that a lot of students don't read the syllabus to find out when papers are due and tests are scheduled. They might not realize a test has come and gone. They miss a few assignment deadlines and their grades fall past the point of recovery. Online students must monitor their own progress.

· ·

"The most important factors are keeping up with the assignment each week and staying focused. Since you really aren't going to class, it's up to you to sign-in on a regular basis and look for feedback and communication from the professors."

Julio Aira Jr.
Master's Student
Business Administration
Nova Southeastern University

· ·

④ Can you learn without a teacher leading you every step of the way?

Successful online students are self-starters. Mark Kretovics, Ph.D., Assistant Professor, Higher Education Administration at Kent State University, uses the metaphor of a fast-food restaurant to illustrate how online students need to learn independently. "When you order a soda at a fast-food place, they give you a cup and you have to fill it up. As an online student, you are invited into the classroom, but it's up to you as to what you take out of the class," he says. In other words, in the online environment, students get a topic of discussion from the professor, but it's up to them to research the topic and analyze, synthesize, and apply the information to the class and then discuss it without a teacher dictating what to do. If you need lots of guidance and are a passive learner, online is not for you. You won't have the motivation of other students sitting next to you in the class or library. The burden is on you to learn the material and keep up with the work.

. . . .

"You are held accountable to do the reading and assignments. It's easy to put them off to the last minute and then have to catch up on three books and twenty-six chapters. I'm sorry, but it's not easy."

Patti Jennings
Bachelor's Student
Library and Information Systems
University of Illinois at Springfield

. . . .

⑤ Do you learn better by seeing or hearing?

This is a critical question. Your learning style plays an important role in how well you will do online. You should determine how you prefer to get information. "Some people really like to learn by reading. Others learn better by listening," notes Steven W. Gilbert, President of The TLT Group, meaning that if most of an online class involves reading text on a screen and you are a "listening learner," you probably won't do as well. Some people learn sequentially—information is given step-by-step and each module builds on the previous one. Learning from textbooks is sequential learning, whereas the Web tends to offer information in a nonsequential way. Some people are hands-on learners who learn best by doing. Students in face-to-face classes usually get information by listening to a professor and reading. While some online classes offer audio and video clips, most of the material is still text-based.

Learning styles also include whether you like to learn alone or with others. Online learning programs offer several different ways to learn so you can match your learning style to the course presentation. Gilbert asks, "If you're a potential student, do you want to find something that matches your learning style, making it easy for you to learn, or do you want to be stretched to learn in other ways?" For the extremely bright student, learning styles are not as relevant, but for those in the middle range, knowing how they learn best and choosing the kind of teaching that suits them best can make a difference.

Some online learning providers recognize that students can have difficulty learning on a computer and build auditory and hands-on elements into their courses. Some have online student resource centers and Web sites where students can find out how they learn best. Even local community colleges or career centers might offer ways to assess your learning style.

. . . .

"If you're an introvert or someone who prefers to work alone and are more productive in an isolated environment, then online courses may be a good fit. But I would say that this is another one of those 'everything in moderation,' since there are benefits derived from all methods of learning."

Edwin R. Watkins
Dual-Master's Student
Telecommunications and Computer Information Systems
University of Denver, University College

. . . .

⑥ How are you at communicating ideas?

Ray Schroeder, Professor Emeritus and Director of Technology-Enhanced Learning and Faculty Associate at the University of Illinois at Springfield, gives presentations about online learning. He likes to ask his audiences to recall their favorite classes from kindergarten to the present and what made them memorable. Was it the textbook? The view out the window? Few respond. Finally, he asks if it was the interaction between the teacher and students and hands fly up. "Learning takes place in the interaction," Schroeder comments. "Otherwise we would do just as well to simply read the book or watch the video to learn."

The interaction that takes place in online classes takes any number of forms: e-mail discussions, listening and responding to teachers via VoIP, or teleconferencing. However, most of the interaction is through text. Some people are better at communicating in written form rather than orally. What online students have to learn is that "you are what you write in class," according to

Claudine SchWeber from the University of Maryland University College. She points out that if your grammar is bad, if you can't communicate ideas, and if you treat discussion boards like text messaging with friends, you won't do well in an online academic environment.

Netiquette is a big factor in online classes. Online students can inadvertently say things they would never say face-to-face to a professor or other students. Angry students can sometimes become quite disrespectful or unacceptably informal when e-mailing teachers. Lori McNabb, Student and Faculty Services Manager at the University of Texas System TeleCampus, mentions a situation in which a student e-mailed a professor with a message that said, "I know my paper is due this Wednesday, but I want to turn it in on Thursday." Unfortunately, the informality of e-mail encourages students to forget how they should communicate with their professors.

· ·

"We must be careful with the tone of our comments on student work. It's important in online teaching to be encouraging and positive."

Cynthia Maxson
English Faculty
Rio Salado College

· ·

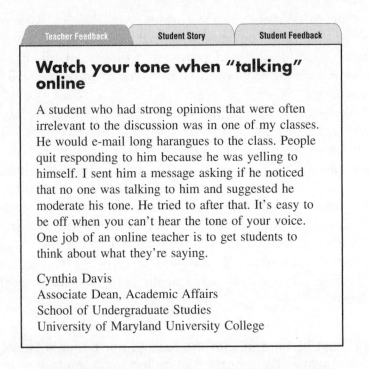

Teacher Feedback   Student Story   Student Feedback

Watch your tone when "talking" online

A student who had strong opinions that were often irrelevant to the discussion was in one of my classes. He would e-mail long harangues to the class. People quit responding to him because he was yelling to himself. I sent him a message asking if he noticed that no one was talking to him and suggested he moderate his tone. He tried to after that. It's easy to be off when you can't hear the tone of your voice. One job of an online teacher is to get students to think about what they're saying.

Cynthia Davis
Associate Dean, Academic Affairs
School of Undergraduate Studies
University of Maryland University College

10 COMMON ONLINE COMMUNICATION BLUNDERS

1. Hitting the submit button instead of reading what you've written.
2. Shooting off e-mails when you are angry, instead of cooling off and thinking about what you're writing.
3. Waiting until 30 minutes before an assignment is due to ask a question.
4. Misinterpreting attempts at humor as personal attacks.
5. Making personal attacks instead of examining ideas.
6. Abbreviating too often or using all capital letters.
7. Failing to address faculty members in a respectful way.
8. Not being assertive enough in introducing yourself to faculty members so they get to know you as a person.

9. Neglecting to follow instructions, so when a teacher says write two paragraphs, you write ten.

10. Getting frustrated and angry and dropping out without trying to clarify the problem with the professor.

❼ Do you have the technical skills and equipment you will need?

Those who develop and use technology to deliver online education don't want to replace geographical limitations with technical limitations. Though there are many cutting-edge technologies to facilitate online teaching, educators do tend to use familiar technology so that no special training is necessary. In most cases, online programs have tutorials and telephone support for students. That said, students need to know some computer jargon. You should know how to "post" an assignment or use a "drop box." Another technical obstacle is low bandwidth. If you need to download graphs or photos that take hours due to a slow dial-up connection, it can get frustrating. "Most computers purchased in the last five years have the speed and memory to support online learning. Some classes require a microphone to be plugged into the computer," notes Ray Schroeder from the University of Illinois at Springfield.

. . . .

"Students are given a Web site to go to and the instructor goes there as well. Students see and hear the instructor and can press a button to indicate they want to speak. All students hear the instructor and each other as if they were in the same room. This uses as little as a dial-up connection and a $400 computer, which is generally within reach of most people who are paying college tuition."

Ray Schroeder
Professor Emeritus, Director of Technology-Enhanced
Learning, and Faculty Associate
University of Illinois at Springfield

. . . .

⑧ Do you have the support of your family?

Once a few papers and assignments are due at the same time or you're deep into a test, you had better be sure your family accepts and supports your decision to be an online student. You need to set aside the time and place to learn, and if your family isn't on the same page, you will run into problems.

. . . .

"Students need to have good time-management skills and work with their syllabi to set their schedules. They need to make sure their families understand that when they are at the computer, they are in class."

Jennifer Rees
Manager, Communication Services
University of Texas System TeleCampus

. . . .

▶ **HOW WILL I KNOW IF I'LL DO WELL AS AN ONLINE STUDENT?**

Online learning providers don't want students to drop out, so they offer several ways for students to find out if they are compatible with the virtual classroom, including self-assessment quizzes on their Web sites. Consider the following:

- Look at the course syllabus so you will know ahead of time what's required. What is the workload? Are assignments due every other day or every two weeks? How many textbooks must you read? Are there many group projects? How is the course graded? Is a sample lesson available?
- Take a quiz to assess how well suited you are to online learning.
- Take only one online class the first time. Gradually add classes, but beware of taking too many at one time.
- Talk to a student adviser and express any concerns or worries about the online environment.

. . . .

"I would recommend taking some of your classes online to get the experience of this type of learning. For a person who is not sure whether to take the class, I would say it's a great learning experience and if the professor is experienced, you will find it to be fun and enjoyable."

Julio Aira Jr.
Master's Student
Business Administration
Nova Southeastern University

. . . .

▶Part VI

WOW! When Do I Start?

Search

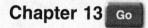

Chapter 13

Choosing an Online Program

Ready to dig into the details and choose the online learning program that best fits your needs and circumstances? Since geographic location is not part of the criteria, you literally have thousands of programs from which to choose. However, you can't depend on name recognition alone. Remember, online programs vary in what they offer and how they deliver education. And price is not a reliable indication of a program's value.

START WITH STATISTICS

The Program's Track Record

An online program can have the glitziest advertising about how easy it is to earn a degree, but its graduation and drop out rates tell the true story. If retention rates are low, it probably means students are not being taught well.

Experience in Delivering Online Classes

It has taken years for online providers to learn how to best design courses, train faculty, and serve online students. Quality institutions continuously learn about and develop new methodologies. Newer online program providers gain from experienced providers, plus a number of organizations provide assistance in designing and implementing online courses. However, setting up the infrastructure and training teachers and administrators for online programs takes time. Some major universities have the name recognition, but do their online programs have the recognition, too?

Number of Students in Classes

In face-to-face classes, you can see how many students the professor has to accommodate. Sometimes in online classes you won't know the student-to-teacher ratio until the teacher doesn't respond to your e-mails because he is sifting through hundreds of e-mails a day. There is a good tip-off, though. Online providers who have a low student-to-teacher ratio will proudly publicize it. Those who cram online students on a teacher's roster will keep it quiet.

Class size also depends on the course material and how it's taught. Online lectures with minimal teacher interaction obviously can and do have more students. Classes with high interaction shouldn't have more than twenty-five to thirty students.

Standards and Practices

When an online provider promotes its standards and best practices for quality online education, there has to be some accountability. Ask about standards the provider has adopted and then check out the organization that awarded them. Diploma mills are quite clever in assigning themselves accreditation and stamps of approval.

WILL THIS PROGRAM MEET YOUR NEEDS?

Does It Specialize in the Courses You Want?

As Janet Poley, Ph.D., President of the American Distance Education Consortium, notes, "Lots of people would prefer Harvard, but plant pathology is not a Harvard specialty." The same is true for students looking for online programs. Some programs are strong in business courses, others in engineering. When it comes to licensing or certification, it's even more critical. If you take courses toward a license or certificate from an out-of-state online provider, make sure the degree, license, or certificate is valid in the state in which you will use it. Ernest Eugster, Ph.D., Academic Director of Computer Information Systems at the University of Denver, University College, suggests that if you take technical classes for industry certification, find out if the courses teach what is currently relevant to that technical field.

· ·

"You can get your M.B.A. from a thousand different places and, for some purposes, it won't matter. For instance, if you're starting your own business or going into the family business, who cares? But if you are 22 and want to get a big-deal job in the financial field, name recognition matters a lot."

Steven W. Gilbert
President
The TLT Group

· ·

What Is the Policy for Transferring Credits?

Transferring credits between institutions has gotten better since online education has become more accepted. However, according to Thomas W. Wilkinson, Director of the Institute for Distance and Distributed Learning at Virginia Polytechnic Institute and State University, "Just because university A offers online courses in English composition doesn't mean that course will transfer to another institution."

Online students in many institutions receive degrees that are no different from those of face-to-face students, so transferring from an institution such as Virginia Tech to another institution wouldn't differ for online or face-to-face students. This extends to online providers in a consortium. But students can't assume that all courses taken at one institution will transfer to another. Lori McNabb, Services Manager at the University of Texas System TeleCampus, suggests talking to academic advisers at the two or three providers to which you're considering transferring credits. One provider might say you can transfer credits from five classes, another might say two. This will affect the cost and length of time to graduate. "Sometimes students think they can go to different campuses and turn in their credits and get a degree. Every campus has limits to the courses they will transfer in," she notes.

What Happens if I Need to Leave a Course Partway Through?

For online students with jobs and families, life sometimes unexpectedly gets in the way of studies and the only way to deal with it is to leave a course. Before enrolling, ask what provisions the program makes if you have to drop a course in the middle. Can you get a refund? What are the policies for readmission?

Does the Online Program Have Services for Students with Disabilities?

A program's brochures, Web site, and course catalog can give you a lot of information on how the program handles accessibility issues. "People with disabilities need to identify themselves," says Jeff Ian Finlay, former Assistant Director of the Center for Media and New Technologies at the University of Maryland University College, now Grants Manager for Montgomery College. Some programs have a disabilities coordinator. Ask about policies and accessibility. What kinds of accommodations can students with disabilities expect, such as taking longer to complete tests?

CONSIDER WHO WILL TEACH YOU

How Do Teachers Respond to Students?

Every teacher has a different teaching style but in online classes, how each teacher teaches is crucial. "Students need guidance and encouragement. That's the professor's job. If students didn't need that, then we could replace all universities with bookstores and Web sites," says Keith W. Miller, Professor of Computer Science at the University of Illinois at Springfield. Student success, in part, depends on the instructor. Ask questions such as "How long have faculty members taught online?" and "How long does it take to get homework back?" and "Do professors answer e-mail frequently?"

. . . .

"If at all possible, students should view a portion of the online course before deciding to take it. They should note the instructor's writing and teaching style and expectations. There should be a clear plan for content presentation, interactivity, communication, and assessment."

Jennifer Freeman
Course Development Team Leader
University of Texas System TeleCampus

. . . .

How Are the Teachers Trained to Teach Online?

Find out how much emphasis a provider gives to training since institutions have very different ways to train, as Melody Thompson, Ed.D., Director of the American Center for the Study of Distance Education and Director of Planning and Research at Pennsylvania State University's Continuing Education, points out. For-profit online institutions usually have control over faculty members and can require their training. However, in institutions with a strong tradition of faculty and/or union control, such training may be suggested but not required.

Are Teachers Certified and Experienced in Their Fields?

Some online providers use adjunct faculty members who are practitioners in their fields. At the University of Phoenix Online, for instance, a marketing class in health administration might have the CEO of a health group or a person running the health-care system of a senior center develop and/or teach the class. Students would work with the CEO to develop a proactive marketing plan so that they not only learn information but use it in real-life situations. Comments Henry T. Radda, Ph.D., Director of the School for Advanced Studies at the University of Phoenix Online, "All of our faculty members are employed elsewhere as leaders in their organizations, whether in health care, education, or business."

HOW IS THE CURRICULUM DEVELOPED?

Don't assume that just because a history teacher is a terrific professor in a face-to-face environment that he or she has any idea how to transfer that same course information to online delivery. The design of an online course is crucial to student success because the physical cues and interaction of a face-to-face class must be built into the online environment. Well-designed courses combine the talents of faculty and professors, hands-on teachers, graphic designers, instructional designers, programmers, animators, and experts in Java™ and Flash.™ All of these components are extremely important in providing successful online learning.

▶ COURSE DEVELOPMENT

What Does a Well-Designed Course Look Like?

- clear organization
- clear goals and objectives
- thorough instructions for all assignments and other course logistics
- instructionally appropriate media (graphics, audio/video, animations, etc.)
- opportunities for interaction
- activities that encourage students to be active learners
- student resources (library, tutoring, technical support, etc.)
- clear content that's easy to read and aesthetically pleasing

What Does a Poorly Designed Course Look Like?

- unclear content organization, unclear navigation
- incomplete or wrong information in the syllabus
- unclear expectations and learning objectives
- incomplete or missing instructions for class participation, homework assignments, etc.
- no clear communication plan
- few opportunities for students to interact with other students, instructors, or the course material itself
- poor content presentation (typos, errors, text-heavy and difficult-to-read materials, technical problems, etc.)
- assistance and/or resources for students are incomplete or missing

(List created by Jennifer Freeman, Course Development Team Leader, University of Texas System TeleCampus)

STUDENT SERVICES MUST BE A PRIORITY

Are Student Services Set Up for Online Students?

Since you probably can't physically walk into an office to get what you need, services for online students are an essential component to your success and satisfaction. Though you have to be more of a self-advocate than a face-to-face student does, the online program you're considering should have someone designated who can help you or point you to someone who can, whether for financial aid, veterans' affairs, or the library. "From the moment students fill out an application for admission, they are assigned an adviser," says Karen M. Lesch, Academic Advisor at Penn State World Campus. To help them feel like they are part of the campus, incoming students get a Penn State sticker, an official degree audit, and the offer of help in selecting courses. The help doesn't end after students are admitted. When students have completed 75 percent of their work for a course, their assigned adviser contacts them to discuss options for their next courses.

Look to see how clear and accessible information on the school's Web site is for prospective and current students. How responsive is the program adviser to your calls or e-mails? Does the program provide toll-free numbers for assistance?

▶ WHAT YOU'LL PROBABLY ASK A STUDENT ADVISER

As a Student and Faculty Services Manager at the University of Texas System TeleCampus, Lori McNabb gets questions from prospective students. Here are some of the more common ones, along with her answers, relative to the University of Texas System TeleCampus.

- **Is the program totally online?** Students want to confirm if they are required to be on campus for some periods of time during the course. In our case everything is done at a distance. Many want to walk in graduation and they can.

- **Is the degree the same?** Students want to be sure their diploma doesn't say something different from diplomas for on-campus students. Our degrees are the same. Occasionally, a campus that is part of a consortium might have a different degree plan.
- **Do I have to take entrance exams?** Students assume that online education is different. Our students must meet identical campus admission requirements and compete for admission with face-to-face students.
- **What degrees do you offer?** Lots of online students think they should be able to get any degree that is offered for face-to-face students. Because of the use of development resources, we cannot offer every on-campus degree online.
- **How do I register?** Our students apply to and are admitted to one of fourteen campuses in the University of Texas System. However, each online program is different.
- **How long will it take to get my degree?** Our degrees are the same number of credit hours whether face-to-face or online. How long it takes to complete the course work depends on whether the student attends full- or part-time.
- **How will I be tested?** Students want to know if they will have to take proctored exams and where their grades will come from. In our courses, you might take quizzes or open-book or timed tests. Many students are not tested but grades are determined by group projects, presentations, and papers.
- **Can you send me information?** People usually want paper. We don't have a paper catalog, as everything is on our Web site.

- **Do you have an Accounting II class?** Some students might need credits to finish a degree somewhere else and are looking for specific courses. All of our course descriptions are on our Web site, as are faculty bios and syllabi. If you want to take a course for transfer and get approval for it, you must be admitted as a non-degree-seeking student.

Will You Be Able to Get Tutoring and Mentoring Online?

Students who have been out of school for a long time have a learning curve to climb. Writing papers does not come easy. They get discouraged and feel they can't keep up with the homework. Foreseeing the problems of many new online students, some online program providers contract out online tutoring services in math or English composition. Others have "dial-a-tutors" available in different languages for students. Online students at Virginia Polytechnic Institute, for example, benefit from a wellness resource center if they are dealing with academic or emotional issues. "We tried to identify just what it is like when a student comes on campus and provide those same support systems to online students," says Thomas Wilkinson.

Does the Library Provide Services for Online Students?

Students on campus spend a lot of time in the library. Digital libraries can be confusing for those not accustomed to them, so quality online programs have librarians dedicated to helping their online students acclimate to their system. What if you're looking for a specific journal? You should be able to get in touch with your institution's librarian to find it online or have it mailed or delivered to you or a library near you. Faculty members teaching online courses should work with the librarians to make sure the resources needed for their classes are available online.

HOW HELPFUL IS THE HELP DESK AND OTHER TECHNOLOGY QUESTIONS

What Are the Technical and Technology Requirements for Online Students?

Some programs send enrolled students a CD with free software or provide all the materials needed to download from their Web site. A few require students to buy supplemental software, such as microphones. Your ISP should be able to support being online for long periods of time. You don't want to be halfway through an essay question and get bumped off because you've timed out. Ask if there's a tech fee. It's usually not much, but you will want to know about any extra fees.

Will You Get Tech Support When You Need It?

Online learning programs can't afford to let students spend hours on the phone trying to fix a software hiccup. Since students tend to do assignments at odd hours, tech support should be available 24/7. "It wouldn't hurt students to call the help desk before they enroll to inquire about the support they can expect," suggests Ray Schroeder, Professor Emeritus, Director of Technology-Enhanced Learning, and Faculty Associate at the University of Illinois at Springfield. "Programs with high course-completion histories generally have reliable technologies. Just as one checks with friends and colleagues about the quality of computers, automobiles, and lawn services, one should check with students who are enrolled in online programs."

▶ A HELPFUL TOOL FROM THOMSON PETERSON'S

Whether you want to get ahead in your career, earn your degree, or pursue a personal interest, continuing your education is always a good decision. At www.petersons.com/onlinelearning you can search for an online degree program using course of study, degree/award level, and on-campus requirements criteria. Or just search by the name of the college or university or keyword. Remember, your education is yours so find the right program for you at www.petersons.com/onlinelearning.

Chapter 13: Choosing an Online Program

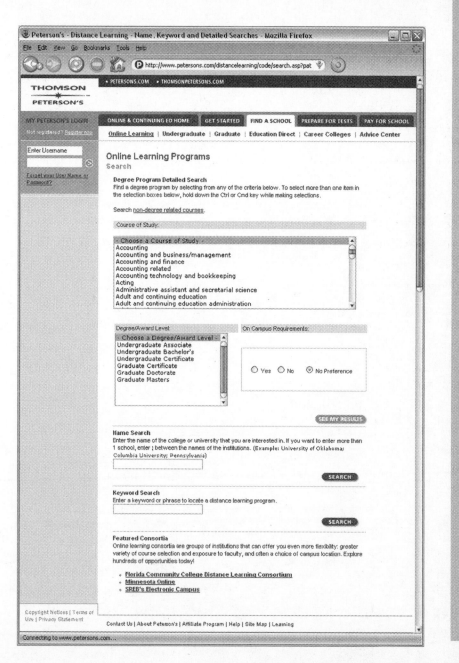

Chapter 14 Go

Accreditation and Diploma Mills

Too bad you can't find an online program that has the course you want at the price you want, click, and you're in. Well, you can, but you also can end up not getting the education you paid for, credits that aren't transferable, or course work that isn't accepted by professional organizations. "I warn students that schools they see on the Internet are not equally good or credible. You can't just cruise the Internet, enter online education, and see what you get," warns Cynthia Davis, Associate Dean of Academic Affairs, School of Undergraduate Studies, University of Maryland University College.

Price should not be the bottom line in your decision. "There is no correlation in quality of education between private and publicly subsidized colleges or the price range between online and face-to-face institutions," says Vicky Phillips, CEO of GetEducated. com, noting that the price range of online programs is "staggering." In a survey her organization conducted in 2004, they found that among 120 accredited online M.B.A.-degree programs with 36 credits and twelve to fifteen courses, the price ranged from $3,000 to $110,000!

Jamie P. Merisotis, President of the Institute for Higher Education Policy, adds that you, the consumer, must take responsibility to determine if an institution will give you the quality education it says it will. "This is a case of caveat emptor," he cautions. The best way to do that is to first make sure the online provider is accredited.

ACCREDITATION COMES FIRST

If you want to learn Web design or photography online, you would obviously check out the organization's background and the credentials of its teachers, but accreditation won't necessarily matter. However, if you are looking to earn a bachelor's degree in economics and then plan to get an M.B.A., "Accreditation is essential," says Celeste M. Sichenze, Professor Emeritus at Northern Virginia Community College and National Coordinator at the American Council on Education. "It gives you some degree of assurance about the organization, regardless of whether it's a distance education provider or a face-to-face institution."

Nonetheless, just knowing if an online program is accredited is still not enough. Sichenze goes on to advise, "Informed learners should know what regional accrediting bodies and national accrediting bodies are and the differences between them." This might sound like more information than you need to know to make a wise decision, but her warning is valid. Anyone can set up an organization and call itself an accrediting agency. It's not that common, but diploma mills (more about them later in this chapter) have been known to create their own accrediting agency and then declare they're accredited. How will you know if "The Approved United States Distance Learning Accrediting Agency," complete with Web site, is legitimate? Hint: No such agency exists—but doesn't it sound official?

Just What Is Accreditation?

The Council for Higher Education Accreditation (CHEA) defines accreditation as "review of the quality of higher education institutions and programs." Within CHEA, private, nongovernmental educational agencies with a regional or national scope have adopted standards for evaluating whether or not colleges and universities provide educational programs at basic levels of quality. Institutions seeking accreditation conduct an in-depth self-study to measure their performance against these standards. The accrediting agency then conducts an on-site evaluation and either awards accreditation or preaccreditation status or denies accreditation.

Periodically, the agency reevaluates each institution to make sure continued accreditation is warranted. Accreditation is not a one-step process. An institution must maintain high standards or face jeopardizing its accreditation status as a result of these periodic evaluations.

Seeking accreditation is entirely voluntary. The initial accreditation process can take as many as five or ten years and it costs money. For that reason, recently established online program providers that are perfectly legitimate may not have been in operation long enough to be accredited. Western Governors University, a virtual university established in 1998, was awarded accreditation candidacy status in 2000 and only received regional accreditation in February 2003.

Who Does the Accrediting?

Accrediting agencies are private, nongovernmental organizations. In other countries, government agencies oversee educational quality. In the United States, authority over postsecondary educational institutions is decentralized. Although there are some national accrediting agencies, each state, not the federal government, regulates educational institutions within its borders and, as a consequence, standards and quality vary considerably.

There are two basic types of accreditation: institutional accreditation and specialized accreditation. Institutional accreditation is awarded to an institution by one of six regional accrediting agencies, such as the Middle States Association of Colleges and Schools, and national accrediting agencies, such as the Distance Education and Training Council.

In contrast to institutional accreditation, specialized accreditation usually applies to a single department, program, or school that is part of a larger institution of higher education. The accredited unit may be as big as a college within a university or as small as a program within a field of study. Most specialized accrediting agencies review units within institutions that are regionally accredited, although some specialized accrediting agencies also accredit institutions.

There are specialized accrediting agencies in nearly fifty fields. Specialized accreditation varies considerably depending on the field of study. In some professional fields, you must have a degree or certificate from a program with specialized accreditation in order to take qualifying exams or be in practice. In others, specialized accreditation has little or no effect on your ability to work in the field. Thus it's critical to find out what role accreditation plays in your field since it may affect both your professional future and the quality of your education.

What Is the Purpose of Accreditation?

If you know an online provider is accredited and by whom, you will know about the provider's quality, whether you can get federal financial assistance and state funds, and if you will be able to easily transfer credits from one school to another.

Quality

Unaffiliated distance learning providers and nonaccredited schools are operating on their own," says Michael P. Lambert, Executive Director of the Distance Education and Training Council. When an institution is accredited, its faculty members, curriculum development, student services, and libraries have met established standards. The institution has shown fiscal stability. In addition, colleges, universities, and employers are more likely to recognize any certificate or degree you earn as a legitimate credential.

Funding

The federal government uses accreditation organizations to ensure students receiving federal loans and grants are attending institutions that maintain high standards of quality. State governments do the same, ensuring that students receiving state loans and grants and going for state licensure examinations in some professional fields are attending institutions with high-quality standards.

Transferring credits

Whether or not you intend to transfer credits from a course or program, accreditation is one major factor the receiving institution takes into consideration. Any credits you earn are more likely to transfer to other regionally accredited institutions, although each institution makes its own decision to transfer credits on a case-by-case basis. For instance, Vicky Phillips, CEO of GetEducated.com, notes, "Accredited institutions don't have to recognize each other's credits. Consumers must be aware that transferability of credits can impact them later on."

▶ WHICH IS BEST: NATIONAL OR REGIONAL ACCREDITATION?

Because the federal government hasn't established a national system, the best form of accreditation is regional. "This is counterintuitive and confusing to consumers," says Vicky Phillips, CEO of GetEducated.com. Remember, no national or federal law requires a college to be accredited by a nationally recognized agency. Unfortunately, most consumers think that national accreditation is better than regional accreditation. Diploma mills play on this assumption. "Diploma mills say they're nationally accredited and, in the minds of the consumer, that's better," states Phillips.

This is not to say that you should dismiss national accreditation organizations. For instance, the Distance Education and Training Council sponsors a nationally recognized accrediting agency, the Accrediting Commission of the Distance Education and Training Council. There are also national accrediting bodies that are discipline based.

HOW TO KNOW WHETHER AN INSTITUTION IS REALLY ACCREDITED

There are many ways to check whether an institution is accredited by a recognized organization. A good place to start is with the Department of Education Web site: www.ope.ed.gov/accreditation/. There you will find a master list of 6,900 postsecondary colleges, universities, and career and trade schools. These schools have been accredited by a recognized accrediting agency or state approval agency recognized by the U.S. Secretary of Education as a "reliable authority as to the quality of postsecondary education," as the Web site states. To help you find out how to spot a fake degree and how to verify an academic institution's credentials, the Federal Trade Commission recently published "Avoid Fake-Degree Burns by Researching Academic Credentials" (available at http://www.ftc.gov/bcp/conline/pubs/buspubs/diplomamills.htm). Another place to look is CHEA's Web site: www.chea.org. This organization lists about 3,000 colleges and universities and encompasses more than sixty national, regional, and specialized accrediting organizations.

WHAT IF AN INSTITUTION YOU'RE CONSIDERING ISN'T ACCREDITED?

As mentioned before, since online programs are still somewhat new, some might either choose to not be accredited or are in the process of becoming accredited. The process takes some time.

How can you make sure a school is legitimate if it is not accredited? First, call the state agency with jurisdiction over higher education in the state in which the school is located. The agency can at least tell you whether or not the school is operating with a legitimate charter and if any complaints have been lodged or legal action has been taken. Second, call the school and ask why it is not accredited and whether the school plans to seek accreditation. If the school tells you it has applied for accreditation, double-check its status with the agency it names. Third, consult with people in your field about the school's reputation and the value of its degree. Don't forget, in some fields, a degree from an unaccredited school or program will bar you from professional licensure and practice.

DIPLOMA MILLS—GET YOUR DEGREE FOR ONLY $500?

By now, *diploma mills* is a well-known term in distance education and in the public mind. What you probably don't know is just how prevalent diploma mills are. "They are a huge business, making huge profits, and people have ample opportunities to run into them on the Internet," says Vicky Phillips from GetEducated.com. When you can buy a diploma for $500 to $2,500 and pay an extra $500 for magna cum laude, that's a diploma mill. They have mushroomed in the online environment. With such varied state regulations, some states have become diploma-mill breeding grounds. Because diploma mills present themselves as viable educational institutions, it is difficult for the less-than-savvy person to differentiate them from legitimate institutions.

When potential students are smart enough to ask an online program provider if it is accredited, diploma mills say yes and point to their Web site. Their Web site says they are accredited, but is it by a recognized accrediting organization? Probably not. Some states are cracking down, but diploma mills just move to another state. Gerald Heeger, President of the University of Maryland University College, notes that, even with stricter government regulations, people looking for online education must take responsibility for themselves. "It's no different from getting a mortgage. You don't go out and borrow money from people you never heard of. You shouldn't get degrees from people you never heard of," he counsels.

Chapter 15 Go

How to Apply

You might think that because you are applying for online and distance education the admittance process is different. It isn't. But don't worry. You will get through admission tests, filling out applications, getting letters of recommendation, writing essays, and transferring credits as so many millions already have.

THE TESTS

You may be anxious about taking an admission test (SAT®, ACT®, GRE®, or one of the professional exams—LSAT®, MCAT®, or GMAT®), but if you apply to a program with that requirement, there is no way of avoiding it. Many undergraduate programs require the SAT or ACT Assessment. Graduate programs often require the GRE, a professional examination, or a Subject Test. Also, if you are not a native speaker of English, you may need to pass the TOEFL® (Test of English as a Foreign Language).

Take heart though. Some programs at community colleges and distance and online learning programs that are specifically designed for adult learners do not require a standardized admission test as part of the application process. For example, if you are applying to the University of Maryland University College (UMUC) to take undergraduate courses, you only need a high school diploma or the equivalent. However, at the University of Texas System TeleCampus, the admission criteria and processes for online offerings are generally the same as for on-site courses. At Virginia Polytechnic Institute, online learners must apply formally for admission to either their undergraduate or graduate degree programs. At Indiana State University, admission requirements vary by program of study.

Predictably, policies get a bit more stringent at the graduate level and vary widely. Students applying to UMUC graduate departments are not required to take an admission test to get into their master's degree and certificate programs. But they must have a regionally accredited bachelor's degree and a GPA of at least 3.0 on a 4.0 scale. At the other end of the spectrum, at Duke University Fuqua School of Business, M.B.A. applicants must have a bachelor's degree or equivalent, company sponsorship, GMAT scores, and TOEFL scores, if applicable.

Once you know which exam you must take, contact the testing service that gives the exam and request registration materials or register online. Each testing service's Web site is given in the following descriptions.

Undergraduate Admission Tests

Bachelor's degree programs that require a standardized admission test usually accept either the SAT or the ACT Assessment; some programs require specific SAT Subject Tests.

The ACT Assessment assesses high school students' general educational development and their ability to complete college-level work. The multiple-choice tests cover four skill areas: English, mathematics, reading, and science. The Writing Test, which is optional, measures skill in planning and writing a short essay. Web site: www.act.org

The SAT is a measure of the critical-thinking skills needed for academic success and assesses how well you analyze and solve problems. Each section of the SAT is scored on a scale of 200 to 800. The SAT includes a Critical Reading, Math, and Writing section, with a specific number of questions related to content. In addition, there is one 25-minute unscored section, known as the variable or equating section. This unscored section may be a multiple-choice Critical Reading, Math, or Writing section. Web site: www.collegeboard.com

SAT Subject Tests are designed to measure knowledge and skills in particular subject areas, as well as the ability to apply that knowledge. Students take the Subject Tests to demonstrate their mastery of five general subject areas: English, History and Social Studies, Mathematics, Science, and Languages. The tests' content evolves to reflect current trends in high school curricula, but the types of questions change little from year to year.

Many colleges use the Subject Tests for admission, for course placement, and to advise students about course selection. Some colleges specify the Subject Tests they require for admission or placement; others allow applicants to choose which tests to take. All Subject Tests are 1-hour, multiple-choice tests. Web site: www.collegeboard.com

Graduate Admission Tests

If you apply to graduate school, you may need to take a graduate admission test, namely the GRE and/or the GRE Subject Tests. The Miller Analogies Test is sometimes required instead of the GRE. In addition, specialized exams are often required for admission to various professional programs.

According to Educational Testing Service (ETS), the **GRE (Graduate Records Examinations)** "measures verbal, quantitative, and analytical reasoning skills that have been developed over a long period of time and are not necessarily related to any field of study." Like the SAT, the GRE is designed to assess whether or not you have the aptitude for higher-level study. Even though the GRE may not have subject area relevance, it can indicate that you are capable of doing the difficult reading, synthesizing, and writing demanded of most graduate students. The test, which is given only on computer, is divided into three separately timed parts: verbal, quantitative, and analytical, and all the questions are multiple choice. A new GRE is expected to be rolled out in fall 2006. Web site: www.ets.org

GRE Subject Tests test your content knowledge of particular subjects. The eight subject area tests are biochemistry, cell and molecular biology; biology; chemistry; computer science; literature in English; mathematics; physics; and psychology. The tests assume a level of knowledge consistent with majoring in a subject or at least having an extensive background in it. Web site: www.ets.org

The Miller Analogies Test (MAT) is a high-level test of mental ability and critical-thinking skills. It has 120 partial analogies and is timed at 60 minutes. The questions cover a broad range of subjects, including vocabulary, literature, social studies, mathematics, and science. Web site: www.harcourtassessment.com/HAIWEB/Cultures/en-US/dotCom/milleranalogies.com.htm

Professional School Exams

Professional graduate programs are likely to require the appropriate graduate admission test: for business school applicants, the GMAT; for law school applicants, the LSAT; and for medical school applicants, the MCAT.

The GMAT (Graduate Management Admission Test) is run by the Graduate Management Admissions Council and administered by Educational Testing Service. It is designed to evaluate basic verbal, mathematical, and analytical writing skills that prospective students have gained from years of work experience and prior education. Web site: www.mba.com/mba

The LSAT (Law School Admission Test) is a half-day standardized test required for admission to all ABA-approved law schools, most Canadian law schools, and many non-ABA-approved law schools. It provides a standard measure of acquired reading and verbal reasoning skills that law schools can use as one of several factors in assessing applicants. The test is administered four times a year at hundreds of locations around the world. Many law schools require that the LSAT be taken by December for admission the following fall. However, taking the test earlier—in June or October—is often advised. Web site: www.lsat.org

The MCAT (Medical College Admission Test) is a standardized, multiple-choice examination designed to assess problem-solving, critical-thinking, and writing skills in addition to the examinee's knowledge of science concepts and principles prerequisite to the study of medicine. Scores are reported in four areas: Verbal Reasoning, Physical Sciences, Writing Sample, and Biological Sciences. Medical college admission committees consider MCAT scores as part of their admission decision process. Web site: www.aamc.org/students/mcat/start.htm

Tests of English Language Proficiency

Because many online students from other countries take courses in U.S. programs, providers often require applicants to take the TOEFL or the TSE (Test of Spoken English) to determine readiness to take courses in English. Both tests are administered by ETS.

The TOEFL is given in computer-based form throughout most of the world. Like the computer-based GRE, the TOEFL does not require previous computer experience. The TOEFL has four sections: listening, reading, structure, and writing and lasts about 4 hours. Web site: www.ets.org/toefl

The TSE evaluates your ability to speak English. During the tests, which take about a half hour, you answer questions presented in written and recorded form. Your responses are recorded; there is no writing requirement. Web site: www.ets.org/tse

▶ **TEST PREPARATION**

Preparation to take admission tests is essential, especially if you've been out of school for a while. Taking practice tests can add points to your score by refreshing both your memory and what the test-taking experience is like. From college admission to career advancement, Thomson Peterson's offers comprehensive test preparation products and services for the SAT, ACT, GRE, GMAT, and TOEFL, as well as civil service and professional licensure and military entrance and advancement. To achieve your best score on admission tests, go to www.petersons.com/clep.

THE APPLICATION

Now that you know about the tests you may have to take, you need to start assembling your applications. Most online admission procedures are fairly simple and forms can be electronically submitted. But don't be fooled by the convenience of online applications. Failing to meet deadlines and following instructions trip up online learners just as easily as they do face-to-face students.

You will likely have to submit a number of items for your application to be considered complete:

- Admission test scores (if required)
- Application form
- High school, undergraduate, or other transcripts
- Letters of recommendation
- Personal essays

In addition, if you seek credit for life experience, an assessment portfolio is required. Some online programs require a personal interview. Art or graphic art online programs require a portfolio.

Many online programs admit students at any time of the year in monthly increments. If you are applying for a bachelor's degree at a regionally accredited university that requires its online students to go through the same process as their face-to-face students, you're in for the long haul. It may take a few months to register for and take standardized tests and to assemble and submit all the necessary forms. If you're an international student, have been out of school for a few years, or are trying to earn credit for work experience, the process can be even more complicated and lengthy. Make sure you know what the deadlines for applications are and start early. Even if you apply to a certificate program or an associate degree program at a community college, a process that is typically less complicated, make sure to begin the application process well before the application deadline.

Use the Application Checklist to keep track of what you need and completion dates. Talk to an adviser for help with the application process and on transferring credits, if that will be part of your application process. Because requirements vary so widely, read all the admission information thoroughly.

▶ APPLICATION CHECKLIST

Item	Program 1		Program 2		Program 3	
	Due Date	Com-pleted	Due Date	Com-pleted	Due Date	Com-pleted
Program Web site reviewed						
Application form downloaded/requested						
Test scores requested						
Transcripts requested						
Transcripts received						
Program adviser contacted						
Review of transferable credits						
Letters of recommendation solicited						
Letters of recommendation follow-up						
Letters of recommendation received						
Personal essay(s)						
Application fee						
Application submitted						
Application follow-up						
FAFSA submitted						
Other financial aid forms gathered						
Financial aid supporting documents						
Financial aid application submitted						

▶ ## TIPS TO GETTING YOUR APPLICATION SMOOTHLY THROUGH THE PROCESS

- Don't rush through filling out the application. Download the application, print it out, and fill it in by hand. Then transfer the information to the online form.
- Sometimes the application form also includes a section for applying for financial aid. However, a completely separate application form for financial aid might be necessary. Be sure you understand what forms you need to submit and to whom, if you are applying for financial aid.
- Do not proofread your application online. Print it out and proof it. You'll be surprised at how many mistakes you find on a paper copy!
- Make sure everything that is asked for is there!

Transcripts

As proof of your academic background, you will need to submit official transcripts from each high school (for undergraduate programs), college, and university you have attended, even if you have taken just one course from an institution. To request official transcripts, contact your high school's guidance office or the registrars of all the postsecondary institutions you have attended.

▶ ## TIPS TO GETTING TRANSCRIPTS

- Be sure to allow two to three months for your request to be processed.
- To save time, find out the fee for each transcript. Then enclose a check for that amount with your written request.
- Since many schools send transcripts directly to the admission offices of the programs to which you are applying, request an unofficial copy for yourself. Use this copy for your own reference during the application process.

- When reviewing your transcripts, look for weaknesses that may need explaining, even if they occurred years ago. For example, a low overall GPA may hurt your chances of acceptance unless you have a good reason for it. Explain any shortfalls in your transcripts in your personal essay, cover letter, or addendum to the application.

Letters of Recommendation

Letters of recommendation are important because they give the members of the admission committee a more personal view of you than is possible from your grades and test scores. Good letters of recommendation can increase your chances of admission—but lukewarm letters, well, they will get you a lukewarm response. Start asking for recommendations a few months before the application deadline.

And how to get these letters of recommendation? First, if particular teachers or professors are still at your alma mater, get in touch and remind them who you are. Then describe what you've done since you were in their classes and what your plans are for school. Include a resume. Tell the instructors what you remember most about the courses you took with them. Most teachers keep their course records for at least a few years and can look up your grades. If you are still near your high school or undergraduate institution, make an appointment to see the teachers or professors in person.

If you have trouble recruiting teachers and professors to recommend you, call the programs to which you are applying and ask about their policies for applicants in your situation. Many programs designed for adult learners, especially professional programs, allow you to use letters from employers. But remember, if you apply to an academic rather than professional program, letters from employers will not carry as much weight as letters from faculty members.

TIPS TO GETTING EFFECTIVE LETTERS OF RECOMMENDATION

- If possible, at least one of your recommendations should be from a teacher or professor, as he or she can best judge you as a potential student. Admission committees consider teachers and professors peers and are more inclined to trust their judgment.
- If you cannot make up the full complement of letters from faculty members or if you are applying to professional programs, ask employers or people who know you in a professional capacity to write references for you. In fact, if you are applying to professional programs, having letters of recommendation from those already practicing in the field is a plus.
- The letter of recommendation forms contain a waiver. If you sign the waiver, you give up your right to see the letter of recommendation. Before you decide whether or not to sign it, discuss the waiver with each person who is writing you a reference. A confidential letter usually has more validity in the eyes of admission committees, and some recommenders will write you a reference only if you agree to sign the waiver.

The Personal Essay

The essays required of applicants vary widely. For some programs, you may have to explain in one or two paragraphs why you want to go to that institution. Or you may have to write on a more creative topic, such as the person who influenced you the most. For graduate business programs, the application may call for two or three, or even more, essays on different topics.

The admission committee gleans a lot of information from *what* you write. But committee members can also tell a lot from *how* you write. If your writing is clear and conveys your ideas effectively, you demonstrate your ability to communicate. If your writing is free of grammatical and spelling errors, you demonstrate your attention to detail.

Looking for essay ideas? How about:

- your personal and professional goals and their relationship to your education
- how you became interested in a particular field and why you think you are well suited for it
- aspects of your life that make you uniquely qualified to pursue study in this field
- experiences or qualities that distinguish you from other applicants
- unusual hardships or obstacles that you've overcome
- unusual accomplishments, whether personal, professional, or academic
- professional experiences that have contributed to your personal growth
- how your skills and personal characteristics will contribute to your success in a distance learning degree program
- what appeals to you about a particular program
- how your interests and strengths match the program's needs

▶ TIPS FOR WRITING A SOLID ESSAY

- Read the instructions for each program's essay. Answer the question posed. Small differences in wording can affect how you approach each essay.
- If instructions say keep it to one page, do so. If instructions say 100 words, stick to 100 words. If the length is not specified, write no more than two pages.
- Write a strong opening paragraph that grabs the reader's attention. Admission committee members might read fifty essays in a day.
- Don't write a boilerplate essay. Use the knowledge you gained from researching the program to explain why you

think the program is a good match. Your reasons should reflect your knowledge of the program.

- Describe your goals, even if you are not exactly sure what you want to do professionally. Indicating that you have a purpose in obtaining your degree shows that you are focused and motivated and have a real sense of the possibilities.

- *Be yourself.* This is the most common advice from admission directors. You want to be accepted by a program that is a good match for you. At the same time, frame your weaknesses in a positive light.

▶ MORE ESSAY HELP

The essay is the primary tool admission officers use to decide among hundreds or even thousands of applicants with comparable experience and academic credentials. In fact, more than one third of the time an admission officer spends on your application is spent evaluating your essay. To stand out, your essay must not only demonstrate your grasp of grammar and ability to write lucid, structured prose, it must also paint a vivid picture of your personality and character, one that *compels* a busy admission officer to admit you. EssayEdge has helped thousands of applicants with marginal test scores and grades articulate their potential and gain admission to the world's top schools. Visit EssayEdge.com and take your personal essay to a new level.

TRANSFERRING CREDITS

Adult students who have earned some college credits during the course of their careers can decrease the time it takes to earn an undergraduate degree by transferring those credits. Many institutions of higher learning accept transfer credits toward a degree. Since each program's requirements vary, check before you enroll to make sure transferred credits are accepted.

"One of the main concerns that is a significant issue for distance learners is the transferability of credits," states Celeste M. Sichenze, Professor Emeritus, Northern Virginia Community College and National Coordinator at the American Council on Education. A student going to a traditional college can't move from campus to campus and expect to easily transfer credits. It's the same with online programs. Students often assume that they can take courses from several institutions and that all those credits will transfer toward a degree program. Although consortia members typically work together to maximize the transferability of credits from one college to another, it is still up to you to ensure that credits earned elsewhere can be applied at your new institution.

What if you have taken courses at an online program that is not recognized or accredited? "This is the number one frustration issue," says Vicky Phillips, CEO of GetEducated.com, speaking of another way people get burned by diploma mills. However, you might have some legitimate reasons to question and change the amount of credit you receive. Phillips suggests that you petition the college if the registrar's office won't accept the credits you want to transfer. But she cautions you must gather ALL your paperwork and be persistent. Check out the Web site for the American Association of Collegiate Registrars and Admissions Officers, www.aacrao.org, for guidance.

EARNING CREDITS BEFORE YOU EVEN ENROLL

Even before enrolling in a college, adult learners may already possess college credits through courses, examinations, or learning acquired in the workplace. Many undergraduate degree programs, especially those designed for adults, give credit for knowledge and skills gained through life experience. Although the knowledge usually comes through paid employment, it can be acquired through volunteer work, company or military training courses, travel, recreational activities, and hobbies and reading.

There is a catch, of course. You must document the specifics of what you have learned. It's simply not enough to say that you learned about marketing while selling widgets for XYZ Company. Instead, you must demonstrate what you learned, for example, by showing plans for a marketing campaign that you created or implemented.

To earn credit for learning from life experience, assemble a file or portfolio of information about your work and other accomplishments. The file may include writing samples, awards, taped presentations or performances, copies of speeches, newspaper articles, official job descriptions, military records, works of art, designs and blueprints, films, or photographs. Your portfolio (or selected portions of the portfolio that are of interest to the college) is then evaluated by an institution's faculty member. In many cases a student can earn as many as 30 credits—one quarter the number needed for a bachelor's degree—as the result of a good portfolio review. Rarely, though, will a portfolio allow you to earn a majority of the credits you need.

How much credit you receive depends on the institution and, within the institution, the policies of internal schools, departments, or programs. "A department might say you will receive no credit," says Thomas Flint, Ph.D., Vice President for Lifelong Learning, Policy and Research at the Council for Adult and Experiential Learning (CAEL). "This is one of the maddening inconsistencies about American higher education. It has led to state legislatures writing state laws requiring acceptance of credits between community colleges and universities." He urges students to ask questions about experiential credit before applying. For more information about assessment opportunities for adult learners, check the CAEL Web site at www.cael.org.

Earning Credits by Taking Exams

It's possible to earn credit for prior learning if you take examinations to assess your knowledge and skills. For example, if you worked in the human resources department of a large organization for years, you may know a lot about human resource management. If you take and pass a college-level exam in human resource management, you can earn credits toward your degree without taking the course or paying tuition. Although some schools have developed their own equivalency exams, most schools accept the results of examinations taken through national programs such as those that follow.

CLEP (College-Level Examination Program®) is the best known of the national equivalency exam programs. It is administered by the College Entrance Examination Board and recognized by 2,900 colleges and universities. Most of the CLEP tests are multiple-choice and some include essays. The test covers what most students take in their first two years of college. CLEP exams are free to military service members. Web site: www. collegeboard.com/clep

Excelsior College Examinations, formerly the Regents College Examination series, are similar to the CLEP. The series consists of about forty subject-area equivalency examinations, which are recognized by nearly 1,000 colleges and universities. Web site: www.excelsior.edu

DANTES Subject Standardized Tests are offered by Thomson Prometric and are accepted or administered at more than 1,900 colleges and universities. Web site: www.getcollegecredit.com/index. html

Credit for Work Training

Since 1974, thousands of employees have earned college credit for selected educational programs sponsored by businesses, industry, professional associations, labor unions, and government agencies. The American Council on Education's College Credit Recommendation Service evaluates such programs according to established college-level criteria and recommends college credit for those programs that measure up to these standards. Check the Council's Web site at www.acenet.edu and select ACE Credit within the program or service on the left. The ACE College Credit Recommendation Service (ACE/Credit) is offered through ACE's Center for Lifelong Learning. Check the list of member organizations (www.acenet.edu/resources/memberdirectory) to determine if you have taken courses or examinations that carry possible college credit. "Oftentimes working adults are required to take courses for their own job advancement and skill refreshers. In addition to getting job experience and training, working adults may also have the added value of possible college credit if their workplace courses have been evaluated by the American Council on Education," says Jo Ann Robinson, Director of the College Credit Recommendation and Transcript Service of the ACE.

Credit for Military Training
Service in the military, specialized training, and occupational experience have the potential to earn college credit. Many military programs have already been evaluated in terms of their equivalency to college credit. The institutions that belong to Servicemembers Opportunity Colleges (SOC) have agreed to assess students' prior learning and accept each other's credits in transfer. To find out more, check the SOC Web site at www.soc.aascu.org.

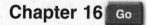

Chapter 16

How to Pay

Despite its convenience and flexibility, online education does indeed cost as much as traditional college education, if not more. While tuition for adult learners is rarely 100 percent covered, the good news is that the federal government does offer educational loans with reasonable interest rates. "Most creditors will tell you that if you have to take out a loan, an educational loan is the best kind of loan to have," advises Bridget McGuire, Executive Director of Financial Aid at Kaplan University.

. . . .

"If students have good credit histories, we can find solutions for them. A bad credit history presents challenges. Federal loans don't require a credit history, but private loans do. Get a free copy of your credit report so you will know what to expect and can take the necessary steps to resolve problems and errors."

Richard Woodland
Director, Financial Aid
Rutgers University, Camden

. . . .

FINANCIAL AID CLASSIFICATIONS

To start, it is helpful to understand some basics about how financial aid can be classified:

By the source of the financial aid:

- The *federal government* is by far the largest disburser of financial aid.
- *State governments* are a source of aid, and some have large financial aid programs.
- *Private sources* of aid include colleges and universities, employers, foundations, service organizations, national scholarship and fellowship programs, home equity loans, and private loan programs.

By the type of aid:

Grants, scholarships, and fellowships do *not* have to be repaid. Scholarships are usually awarded to undergraduate students and fellowships are awarded to graduate students.

Loans are awards that *do* have to be repaid with interest, either while you are in school or after you leave school.

Work-study awards are monies you earn through part-time work in a federal aid program.

Reimbursements, which are generally from employers, repay what you've already spent on tuition.

By the reason you are awarded aid:

Need-based aid is awarded on the basis of your financial need. It may take the form of grants, loans, and/or work-study.

Merit-based aid is awarded on the basis of academic merit, regardless of financial need.

▶ FINANCIAL AID JARGON

As you figure out more about financing your education, you'll run across some terms that may be unfamiliar to you. Let's get familiar with them now.

- *Enrollment status* pertains to whether you are enrolled full-time, three-quarter time, half-time, or less than half-time in a degree or certificate program. Your enrollment status affects your eligibility for most types of aid.
- *Expected Family Contribution (EFC)* is the amount you and your family are expected to contribute to the cost of your education per academic year. If you are a dependent, "family" means you and your parents; if you are independent, it means you (and your spouse, if you are married).

- *Cost of attendance* is the total cost of attending a particular school for an academic year, including tuition, fees, living expenses, books, supplies, and miscellaneous expenses.
- *Financial need* is the amount of money you need in order to cover your expenses at your school. It is calculated by subtracting your EFC from your cost of attendance.

FEDERAL FINANCIAL AID

Most of your financial aid is likely to come from the federal government, which provides need-based aid in the form of grants, work-study programs, and loans.

- *Pell Grants* do not have to be repaid and are awarded to undergraduate students (with no prior degree) on the basis of need, even if they are enrolled less than half-time.
- *Federal Supplemental Educational Opportunity Grants* are awarded to undergraduates (with no prior degree) with exceptional financial need, even if they are enrolled less than half-time.
- *Federal Work-Study Program* provides part-time jobs in public and private nonprofit organizations to both undergraduate and graduate students demonstrating financial need. The government pays up to 75 percent of the student's wages and the employer pays the balance.
- The *Federal Family Education Loan (FFEL) Program* and the *William D. Ford Direct Loan Program* (commonly called *Stafford Loans*) allow students to borrow if they are enrolled at least half-time and have remaining costs after Pell Grant funds and aid from other sources are subtracted from their annual cost of attendance. Depending on remaining financial need, these loans may be subsidized (no interest while in school) or unsubsidized (interest accrues while in school). There are

overall loan limits in place for these federal loan programs, based on year in school.

- *Perkins Loans* are available to both undergraduate and graduate students (full-time or part-time) who demonstrate exceptional financial need.

To apply for federal aid, you must file the Free Application for Federal Student Aid (FAFSA). You can apply online at www.fafsa. ed.gov or by filing the paper application available from any financial aid office. You will need a PIN (which serves as your electronic signature) to file on the Web; PINs are easily obtainable at www.pin.ed.gov.

The most up-to-date information about federal financial aid programs can be found at the U.S. Department of Education's Web site, www.ed.gov/studentaid, or by calling 1-800-4-FEDAID. The U.S. Department of Education's booklet, *The Student Guide*, is an excellent resource on all federal aid programs and is available online at http://studentaid.ed.gov/students/publications/ student_guide/index.html or from any institution's financial aid office.

Are You Eligible for Federal Financial Aid?

Your financial need is just one criterion the federal government uses to determine whether or not you are eligible to receive need-based federal financial aid. In addition, you must:

- have a high school diploma or GED or pass a test approved by the Department of Education;
- be enrolled in a degree or certificate program;
- be enrolled in an eligible institution;
- be a U.S. citizen or eligible noncitizen;
- have a Social Security number;

- register with the Selective Service, if required; and
- maintain satisfactory academic progress once you are in school.

Is the Institution You're Considering Eligible for Federal Financial Aid?

An institution's accreditation status affects its eligibility to participate in federal financial aid programs. If you plan to enroll in a regionally accredited traditional college or university, you can safely assume that the institution is eligible to participate in federal aid programs. However, because institutions do have the discretion to exclude specific programs, check to see if the school disperses federal aid to students enrolled in the programs in which you are interested.

In addition, in order to participate in federal financial aid programs, an institution of higher learning must fulfill certain criteria established by Congress. The federal government has recently relaxed some of the regulations governing distance education programs, and more changes are likely to occur in the next few years as online learning continues to grow. For more information, contact colleges directly or check the U.S. Department of Education's Web site at www.ed.gov.

Once you've confirmed the eligibility of an institution and program, research the federal aid programs in which they participate. Not all schools participate in all federal aid programs.

An Ongoing Debate That Could Affect Your Federal Financial Aid

The rules governing federal aid were originally created to prevent fraud and ensure that funds would be provided to students at schools that met certain standards. However, with the growth of distance education, these regulations are increasingly becoming obstacles to providing aid to students at legitimate, albeit "innovative," institutions. "Our financial aid laws made sense forty years ago when college students were 18-year-old dependents. But today's college students are adults. The efforts to change these laws are positive," says Vicky Phillips, CEO of GetEducated.com.

Congress has established the Distance Education Demonstration Program under the direction of the Department of Education. The federal law states that if academic institutions offer more than 50 percent of their courses through distance or online education, the institution is not eligible for federal financial aid. Online learning programs often refer to this as the "50 percent rule." However, the federal government also recognized that distance and online education was growing and that if this law were to remain in effect, many financially needy students would be ineligible for financial aid. In order to investigate the validity of online and distance learning, the Demonstration Program gave waivers to a selection of educational institutions, including nine for-profit institutions (including five that are publicly traded); seven private, nonprofit institutions; four public universities; one public system; and three consortia.

"If the 50 percent rule goes away, it will be a recognition that online learning is here to stay and that there are other ways to deliver education, given the technology, to students who aren't all physically in one location," notes Tim Lehmann, Director of Financial Aid at Capella University. "This will free up anybody to engage in courses around the world." The Demonstration Program is still being debated in Congress. Eventually, it will provide a basis for revising current rules and regulations for online and distance education providers. Get more information at the Department of Education Web site: http://www.ed.gov/programs/disted/index.html.

STATE FINANCIAL AID

Financial aid varies a great deal from state to state and can change from year to year, which presents many complicated situations for online students. Many states limit their state financial aid to state residents attending school in-state. Some states offer aid to residents who attend school elsewhere and some offer aid to students who attend school in their state, regardless of their residency status. "Kaplan is technically located in Davenport, Iowa," says Bridget McGuire. "Our students currently qualify to get state grants from Iowa and other states like Vermont, Rhode Island, and Michigan. However, they don't currently qualify if they're from Florida, Georgia, or Pennsylvania."

Before making final decisions on which program to attend, you will want to see if your state or the state in which the institution is located is qualified for state financial aid. Contact your state higher education office directly to find out what's available and if you are eligible to apply.

. . . .

"We're seeing the evolution of the states' understanding of online as more mainstream. This is an area where the law is catching up to technology. The states will have to look at what it means to approve a virtual campus and maintain consumer protection."

Tim Lehmann
Director, Financial Aid
Capella University

. . . .

INSTITUTIONAL AND PRIVATE SOURCES OF FINANCIAL AID

Colleges and universities are second only to the federal government in the amount of financial aid disbursed yearly. Many award both need-based and merit-based aid to deserving students. To find out more about the types of aid schools offer, contact their financial aid office.

National and local organizations, including foundations, nonprofit organizations, churches, service and fraternal organizations, professional associations, corporations, and unions, offer scholarships, grants, and low-interest loans to students. You probably won't find many of these offerings specifically for online or distance education students but online students are eligible to apply regardless. "Scholarships are often more specific to a career or ethnic background," notes McGuire. "Most scholarships are for accredited institutions. That's the bigger sticking point, not so much whether it's online." But check this out: Chela Financial, Inc., awards scholarships specifically for distance education students. You can find them at http://www.chelastudentloans.org/.

ALTERNATIVE LOAN PROGRAMS

In addition to the federal loan programs, private alternative loan programs are worth some investigation. Most private loan programs disburse funds based on your creditworthiness rather than your financial need. The college's financial aid office is the best source of information on alternative loan programs.

A home equity loan or line of credit can be an attractive financing alternative to private loan programs. Some of these loans are offered at low rates and allow you to defer payment of the principal for years, while also offering attractive tax advantages.

Internships with organizations outside the university can provide money, as well as practical experience in your field. As an intern, you are usually paid by the outside organization, and you may or may not get college credit for the work you do.

If you work full-time and attend school part-time, your employer may reimburse you for part or all of your tuition. Check with your human resources office for more information.

Whatever you do, do not use your credit cards to borrow money for school on a long-term basis. The interest rates and finance charges are high and the balance will grow astronomically. Credit cards are useful to pay tuition and fees if you can pay the balance in full, expect a student loan to come through shortly, or expect your employer to reimburse your costs. Otherwise, avoid using them!

TAX BENEFITS

Whether or not you receive financial aid, there are many recently enacted tax benefits for adults who want to return to school. In effect, these tax cuts provide financial aid support indirectly through the tax system.

- *The HOPE Scholarship Tax Credit* Students whose adjusted gross income falls within certain limits receive a 100 percent tax credit for the first $1,000 for the first two years of college. The maximum credit is $1,500 per year.
- *The Lifetime Learning Tax Credit* A family may receive a 20 percent tax credit for the first $10,000 of tuition and required fees paid each year. The maximum credit is $2,000 per year, available for an unlimited number of years.
- *The Tuition and Fees Tax Deduction* This deduction can reduce the amount of your taxable income by as much as $4,000 per year. You do not need to itemize your deductions to take advantage of this program. In general, eligibility is limited to Adjusted Gross Incomes of under $65,000 for single individuals and $130,000 for married taxpayers.
- *Individual Retirement Accounts (IRA)* Taxpayers can withdraw funds from an IRA, without penalty, for their own higher education expenses or those of their spouse, child, or even grandchild.

- *State Tuition Plans* When a family uses a qualified state-sponsored tuition plan to save for college, no tax is due in connection with the plan until the time of withdrawal.
- *Tax-Deductible Student Loan Interest* The student loan interest deduction allows students or their families to take a tax deduction for interest paid in the first sixty months of repayment on student loans.
- *Tax-Deductible Employer Reimbursements* If you take undergraduate courses and your employer reimburses you for education-related expenses, you may be able to exclude up to $5,250 of employer-provided education benefits from your income.
- *Community Service Loan Forgiveness* This provision excludes from your income any student loan amounts forgiven by tax-exempt charitable organizations or educational institutions for borrowers who take community-service jobs that address unmet community needs.

For more detailed information, check out the National Association of Student Financial Aid Administrators (NASFAA) Web site at www.nasfaa.org.

▶ **MAKING THE MOST OF YOUR FINANCIAL AID APPLICATION**

- *Don't apply late for financial aid.* High school students going to college don't make this mistake as frequently because they have guidance counselors reminding them about deadlines. Adult online learners, who are on their own, tend to put financial aid at the end of the process. Financial aid, transferring credits, and researching the right program should be concurrent processes.

- *Pay attention to details.* Financial aid entails paying attention to directions. A figure left out here or there can bog down the processing of an application.
- *Follow up with the financial aid office.* You can't assume that because you're submitting a form via e-mail attachments or fax that it got there. Get contact information from the financial aid office and make sure the people who are processing your applications got them.
- *Before applying for financial aid, make sure the online program is accredited.* No accreditation, no federal financial aid. It's as simple as that. The Department of Education's Office of Postsecondary Education maintains a database, the Institutional Accreditation System, of about 6,900 accredited schools and programs. Plug in the name of an institution and you will know if it is accredited. Go to http://ope.ed.gov/accreditation/.
- *Don't try to get through the entire financial aid process completely online.* It might seem easier to fill in forms, hit send, and that's it. Financial aid is complicated and many online programs have financial aid counselors to guide you through the process and help maximize your financial aid resources. But you have to ask for this help and the more specific and detailed your questions, the better your results will be.
- *Don't drop classes too quickly.* Full-time is generally considered to be 12 credits. If you sign up for 12 credits and then drop a class, your financial aid could be affected.
- *Persistence pays.* Be diligent in your search for funds. You may have to spend time researching sources of financial aid and filling out applications. You may have to borrow money and simplify your lifestyle to cut expenses. But remember, if you are persistent, you can—and will—find the financial help that you need.

NOTES

NOTES

NOTES

NOTES

NOTES

NOTES

NOTES